TURNER AND BYRON

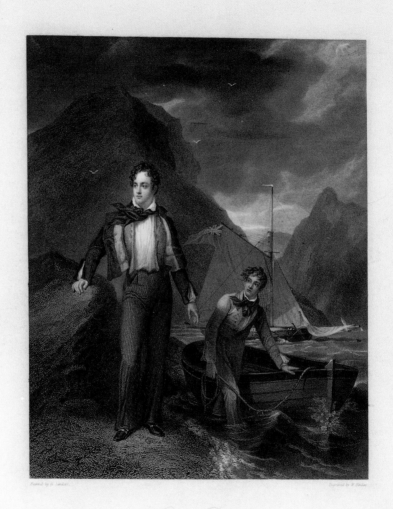

Painted by H. Landseer   *Engraved by H. Linton*

Lord Byron
at the age of 19.

Engraved from the original Picture in the possession of John Cam Hobhouse Esq.r M.P.
to whom this plate is respectfully dedicated

London Published Dec.r 1st 1832 by Murray, Albemarle Street, & J. & F. Tallis, St John's Street, West Smithfield.

DAVID BLAYNEY BROWN

Turner and Byron

TATE GALLERY

Exhibition sponsored by TSB Group plc

Front cover
Venice, the Bridge of Sighs RA 1840 (detail, no.38)

Frontispiece
William Finden **Lord Byron at the Age of 19** (no.41)

ISBN 1 85437 097 9 (paper)
ISBN 1 85437 102 9 (cloth)

Published by order of the Trustees 1992
for the exhibition of 3 June – 20 September 1992
Published by Tate Gallery Publications, Millbank, London SW1P 4RG
© Tate Gallery 1992 All rights reserved
Designed by Caroline Johnston
Typeset in Baskerville by Status Graphics, London
Printed in Great Britain by Pegasus, Mitcham, Surrey

Contents

FOREWORD

Turner's concern with literature was lifelong and profound, and the art of poetry held a special place in his affections. *Turner and Byron* is the second of two exhibitions in the Clore Gallery to explore Turner's relationship with poetry. The first, *Painting and Poetry*, presented in 1990, centred upon his poetic interests and efforts in the earlier part of his career, when the influence of the Augustan poets of the previous century, Alexander Pope and James Thomson, was paramount. Turner's love for these – yet more evidence, if it were needed, of the rooted conservatism that lay beneath his apparently remorseless quest for originality of expression – was matched only by Byron, whose own early work was indelibly stamped with Augustan imagery, rhythm and wit. It is fitting that this second exhibition on a poetic theme should be devoted to Turner's connections with Byron, for of all the great poets of his own day, it was Byron who took over from the Augustans as the poet who best matched and anticipated Turner's own imagination.

Childe Harold's Pilgrimage, published from 1812, introduced Turner to a vision of the modern world that mirrored his own search for a historically resonant and morally didactic art of landscape; what Byron called 'the truth of *history* … and of *place*' was also Turner's truth. The paintings which Turner exhibited on Byronic themes and with quotations from *Childe Harold,* and which form the centrepiece of this exhibition, take us from the horrors of Waterloo to the radiant landscape of the Rhine valley, and from Venice to Rome; they are as varied and contrasted in setting, mood and message as Byron's poetry. Nor was Turner alone in recognising the relevance of Byron's work to his own. For publishers and engravers, Turner was the logical choice to illustrate Byron – not so much the narratives and incidents in his poetry which others were better fitted to render, but the poet's own travels, and the landscapes in which the drama of his life had been played out. For their generation, Turner's were the definitive realisations of the Byronic world, reproduced in the most popular and affordable edition of the poet's life and works. These form the second main focus of the exhibition. Other displays illuminate the circle in which painter and poet moved, demonstrate the more common contemporary approaches to Byronic illustration, and trace Turner's Continental travels in Byron's footsteps.

To all our lenders, headed by Her Majesty the Queen, we owe our deep gratitude for contributing so many important works to this exhibition. We are specially honoured, and delighted, to be able to show here a 'new' and unpublished portrait of Byron, and a fine watercolour by Turner not seen for more than a century. For their patience and generosity during the preparation of the exhibition, David Brown would like to extend particular thanks to John Murray and Virginia Murray, who freely placed the archives of Byron's publisher at his disposal. He has also received valuable assistance from Iain Bain, Gerald Burdon, Luke Herrmann, Evelyn Joll, Caroline Knox, Christopher Lloyd, Dr Jan Piggott, Cecilia Powell, Dudley Snelgrove, Fani-Maria Tsigakou, Rosalind Turner and Robert Woof.

We are especially pleased to be working with TSB Group plc, our sponsor, on this exhibition, as well as a series of annual displays which will examine the work of William Blake. TSB have been exceptionally thoughtful in funding these exhibitions which help to promote scholarship on the permanent collection of the Tate Gallery to a wide range of Gallery visitors.

Nicholas Serota
Director

Sponsor's Foreword

The *Turner and Byron* exhibition demonstrates the affinity between two of the most influential British figures of the nineteenth-century Romantic movement. Europe was a source of inspiration for both the painter and the poet and the exhibition is aptly staged at a time when Britain's role in Europe is at the forefront of our minds.

TSB Group plc is delighted to affirm its continuing commitment to the arts through this sponsorship and to be supporting the Tate Gallery in its role as the national gallery of British art. We hope that as many visitors as possible from both Britain and overseas will take pleasure from viewing this notable exhibition.

Sir Nicholas Goodison *Chairman*
TSB Group plc

TURNER AND BYRON: INTRODUCTION

PAINTER AND POET

'Why say the Poet and Prophet are not often united?', Turner asked the antiquary John Britton from Farnley Hall in November 1811; 'for if they are not they ought to be'.[1] His words were perhaps themselves prophetic, for early the next year the first canto of Byron's *Childe Harold's Pilgrimage* was published, bringing to centre stage the poet who was to be the most vital of the guiding spirits of the age. For all the Romantics, Byron would be a touchstone – not only a great poet, but a wandering, free, revolutionary spirit to whom they might look for emotional or political courage, to whose condition they might aspire or in which they might recognise a portion of themselves, or from whose aberrations they might recoil with exquisite frissons of moral disgust. To read his poetry, or to follow the inspiring or shocking events of his life, was almost a species of the Sublime. His death at Missolonghi just twelve years later, in 1824, was felt throughout Europe hardly less powerfully than Napoleon's, and no author had so well expressed the melancholy ambivalences and the passionate yearnings of the Continent in the years after the Emperor's fall.

Byron's impact on the creative arts was phenomenal, and hardly needs rehearsal here. Quite apart from the reverberations that he and his work created in the world of literature, it is well known that Berlioz, Schumann and Tchaikovsky transposed the restless souls of his most compelling self-portraits, Childe Harold and Manfred, into music, while Delacroix was the greatest and most prolific of his many distinguished interpreters in paint. 'Rappelle-toi, pour t'enflammer éternellement, certains passages de Byron', Delacroix wrote after the poet's death. It was left to Constable – hostile critic among painters as Southey was among poets – to express the opposite view while acknowledging the inevitability of Byron's influence; 'the deadly slime of his touch still remains'.

Byron had commanded the attentions of painters and illustrators from early in his brief and hectic career. He was by far the most popular of all the Romantic poets as a subject for art. His works were seized upon almost as soon as they were published, and remained a staple for most of the century, despite all vicissitudes in his critical reputation. The dramatic nature of the poems, their strongly visual descriptions and powerfully characterised heroes provided vital and stirring images to challenge the greatest painters, while their equal appeal to the overheated emotions of the album and keepsake readers inspired whole galleries of sentimental prints – what Thackeray was to describe as 'that unfortunate collection of deformed

Zuleikas and Medoras'. Byron offered something for everyone, and the iconography of the poetry, and indeed of Byron himself and of 'Byronic Man' in which the poet and his heroes merged, is vast.

Turner, then, was by no means alone in turning to Byron for inspiration and quotation, and as the modern poet who best expressed or underlined his own ideas. Yet among British artists, his response to Byron was outstanding. The series of paintings he made on Byronic themes or exhibited with quotations from the poet do not, it must be admitted, match Delacroix's in number or always in intensity of feeling, but they amount to a roll-call of some of his most impressive pictures, from the 'Field of Waterloo' (no.35) of 1818 to 'Approach to Venice' (no.39) of 1844. He was, moreover, the most distinguished and prolific of Byron's illustrators, whose designs adorned what was, in his lifetime, the prime edition of the poet's life and works. Besides these, there are many others that are, in Andrew Wilton's telling phrase, 'irradiated with the glow of Byronic reminiscence',[2] and others still whose appeal for their first patrons or purchasers would have rested very largely on their realisation of places and ideas familiar from Byron's poetry.

It is curious, therefore, that Turner's long engagement with Byron has never been the subject of special study. His Byron paintings have not been assessed as a group, and the history of his published illustrations has usually been given in an abbreviated or very inaccurate form. Perhaps this has been as much the result of Byron's critical standing for much of our century, as of any prevailing winds in 'Turner studies'. It should be remembered that until the 1940s even Delacroix's Byron subjects were hardly studied as a group,[3] and during a period when Byron's flame had burned low, it was doubtless all too easy to regard Turner's use of Byron as no more than the application of a facile or superficial gloss to his own ideas. Reassessments of Byron and Turner proceeded in the 1970s – Francis Berry's landmark lecture on 'The Poet of Childe Harold', which redeemed Byron's forceful narrative line, his confident conviction, from the strictures of a generation reared on the tentative equivocations and hesitant questionings of T.S. Eliot, was given in 1974,[4] the same year as the great Turner bicentenary exhibition at the Royal Academy. Yet the rehabilitation of them both produced little consideration of them together.

A large part of the reason must lie in the absence of any personal connection between painter and poet. One looks in vain for evidence of a meeting, and had one taken place, it is unlikely that they would have got on. Differences of age and class would have intruded too far. Byron was a schoolboy during the first euphoric years of Turner's success, and an undergraduate when Turner first attracted serious criticism. By the time Turner began to take Byron seriously, and to identify his vision as significantly close to his own, Byron had based himself abroad; and by the time Turner began illustrating the poetry in earnest, the poet was dead. The circumstances of Turner's connections with Byron were thus very different from those governing his associations with other major poets of his time, Samuel Rogers, Walter Scott, Thomas Moore or Thomas Campbell. These were, in varying degrees, his friends, or on occasion his hosts, and when he came to illustrate their work, the enterprise was a collaboration between himself, the poet and their publisher or engraver. With Byron, he dealt at second hand, guided by his own impressions of the poetry, a common sense of history or place, the requirements of publishers or the promptings and recollections of the poet's friends. There is, therefore, no solid personal history to be told of Turner and Byron – only Turner's Byronic work. This alone richly deserves exhibition and study. Beyond it lies a tantalising emptiness, its darkness illuminated by the occasional coincidence, by shared acquaintances or crossings of paths, inviting speculation but remaining in the end mysterious.

Did the two men ever meet? Would they even have sought each other out? Turner's considerable interest in poetry did not result in a comprehensive range of friendships among modern poets – his lack of awareness of Wordsworth, Keats and Coleridge is as striking as his intimacy with Scott or Rogers. On the other hand his unconcern for the Lake Poets, along with his reverence for the Augustans, would have much endeared him to Byron. For his part, Byron did not seek the company of painters, and had no natural love of art, rather affecting a certain John Bullish philistinism. Passing hurriedly over the treasures of Florence in *Childe Harold* he made his characteristic claim

> I have been accustom'd to entwine
> My thoughts with Nature rather in the fields
> Than Art in galleries

and in his notes to the Greek passages of the poem, declared 'I am not a collector or admirer of collections'. It is hard to imagine Byron haunting the Royal Academy or the British Institution – although Constable spotted him at a reception at the latter during its Reynolds exhibition in 1813 – and patrons and connoisseurs were among the inhabitants of the fashionable world with whom he felt least at home. Yet he admired Thomas Lawrence, using his work as an agent of comparison in his neo-Augustan satire on bathos in the arts, *Hints from Horace*, written in Athens in 1811, and admitting in 1821 that the pleasure of conversing with such interesting people as Lawrence was among the main benefits of fame. He fully subscribed to the fashionable passion for Canova ('Such as the great of yore, Canova is today'), commissioned Richard Westall and lent to his one-man exhibition in Pall Mall in 1814, and was intrigued by Fuseli.

With one artist – albeit a lapsed one – Byron did form a special friendship. This was Richard Belgrave Hoppner, the second son of the portrait painter John Hoppner who had given Turner valuable support in his early career, and was a close friend of Byron's literary mentor, William Gifford. Richard Hoppner had first followed in his father's footsteps, but then turned to diplomacy, becoming in 1814 British Consul in Venice. When Byron moved there in 1817, first to lodgings in the city and then to the Palazzo Mocenigo (nos.8, 9), he got to know Hoppner well, riding with him daily on the Lido sands and entrusting him with some of his business affairs and for a time, the care of his daughter Allegra. Byron found him a good listener with an 'acute and original' mind, and 'besides a thoroughly good man'. It has been suggested that, when Turner arrived in Venice for a few days in September 1819, Hoppner would have been well placed to introduce him to Byron, but in fact he was away on a visit to Switzerland, and was then rather distanced from Byron by his disapproval of the poet's new paramour the Countess Guiccioli. Moreover, Byron had now based himself with the Countess at his villa on the Brenta, and Turner was very fully occupied during his brief first visit, so it seems unlikely that either would have found the time to make the other's acquaintance.

Turner and Byron are shown together, with a number of their mutual connections, in Charles Mottram's large print after a design by the young John Doyle (no.4). The scene is one of those famous breakfast parties given by Samuel Rogers at 22 St James's Place, and the date is said to be 1815. Here, in all its sparkling diversity, is the circle in which painter and poet moved, and although the print is clearly imaginary, depicting Rogers's regular guests rather than a particular occasion, this room would have been as likely a setting as any for a meeting. It was Rogers who first guided the young Byron through London's literary and political society in 1811, and it was in his house, in November that year, that Byron and Thomas Moore first met, and turned 'decided hostility to decided friendship'. Turner may well have known Rogers before their connection is documented, in the early 1820s, and he certainly knew Moore by 1819, for they met in Rome – very soon, that is, after Moore had visited Byron in Venice and been presented with the poet's memoirs.

In London, Turner and Byron could only have come across each other between the last months of 1811 and late April 1816. It was not until 1812, following the first publication of *Childe Harold*, that Byron truly became a social lion; he had followed the considerable notoriety of his satire, *English Bards and Scotch Reviewers*, published in 1809, with a tour of Portugal, Spain, Gibraltar, Malta, Albania and Greece, and on his return had spent some months at his Nottinghamshire estate, Newstead. The period up to 1816 witnessed the brief but tempestuous span of Byron's London life – his affairs with Lady Oxford and Lady Caroline Lamb among others, his courtship and unhappy marriage to Anna Isabella Milbanke, and financial dramas and debts; and to set against all this, the fame added by his narrative poems *The Giaour* and *The Bride of Abydos* (1813) and *The Corsair* and

Lara (1814) to the huge success of *Childe Harold. The Siege of Corinth* and *Parisina* were written in 1815; April that year brought the famous meeting with Walter Scott in their publisher John Murray's rooms in Albemarle Street; and in May he became an active member of the Management Committee of the Drury Lane Theatre. By April 1816 his marriage was over, and, amidst a cataclysmic scandal, he left England for good on the twenty-fifth of the month.

Something of this must have come to Turner's attention, and might have been discussed with a mutual acquaintance, the author Henry Gally Knight – also, it seems, a friend of Turner's colleague, the watercolourist James Holworthy. In the summer of 1816, Knight invited Turner to stay at his Yorkshire estate, Langold Hall near Rotherham, and that year Turner exhibited two substantial pictures of the temple at Aegina, based originally – together with a drawing for the *Liber Studiorum* (no.25) – on a sketch Knight had made in Greece in 1810 (see no.26). Knight may well have bought one, which Turner seems to have had in hand since 1814, and their discussions of it could easily have been spiced with talk of Byron, then so much in the news, for Knight and the poet had known each other at Trinity College, Cambridge, and had met in Athens in 1810 and again at Cadiz. They were at first on friendly terms, and when in 1813 Knight was finishing the first of several Oriental poems, *Phrosyne: A Grecian Tale*, he had understandably asked Byron's advice. Turner must also have been shown the poem in manuscript, for although it was not published until 1817, the foreground figures in one of his 1816 paintings were clearly inspired by it. *Phrosyne* was followed by other exoticisms; Knight wrote *Ilderim: A Syrian Tale* in 1816, and *Alashtar: An Arabian Tale* was published with *Phrosyne* the following year. Byron had looked rather gently on Knight's first efforts, even remarking *de haut en bas* that his own similar scenarios, for example in *The Giaour*, had been created 'quite unintentionally'. But he soon lost patience with Knight's reworkings of a vein he had himself made popular; of *Phrosyne* and *Alashtar* he wrote to Murray in 1817 that 'I shall clean my teeth with one, and wipe my – not shoes with the other ', and by 1820 had decided that Knight 'writes like a Country Gentleman – for the County Newspaper'. 'I would rather', he added on another occasion, 'be a Galley-Slave than a Galley Knight – so utterly do I despise the middling mountebank's mediocrity in everything but his income'.[5]

Knight, then, was not ideally placed to bring painter and poet together, but he does suggest at least a tenuous link through their interest in Greece and the Orient at this period – a mutual concern that must be discussed again. There is no way of knowing just how and when Turner first became aware of Byron's poetry, but this was only one of a number of coincidences of interest that would have commended it at once. Turner's love for poetry doubtless led him to new work as it appeared, and the combination of topical allusions and Augustan rhythm in such works as *English Bards and*

Scotch Reviewers and *Hints from Horace* would have appealed to him very strongly; in Byron he would have recognised that devotion to the eighteenth century that he had been striving to express in his own halting verses, and a tonic impatience with cant, pomposity and inflation – indeed Pope's famous phrase from his *Essay on Criticism* (1711), 'what oft was thought, but n'er so well expressed', could stand for Turner's response to Byron.

Satire was of course a favourite medium of the Augustans, but this was not its only appeal to Byron and Turner. Their preoccupation with it was sharpened by the tone and origin of the criticism they themselves were receiving. Despite the lack of evidence for actual contact between them, there are aspects of their common experience that seem to go beyond mere coincidence – or at least emphasise how much they belonged to a world whose shared values and bones of contention were the same; it is especially interesting to consider the critical climate in which Turner was operating, and Byron was establishing and defending his reputation by about 1809. Despite their conservative tendencies, both men were being attacked as subversive and in language that was remarkably similar. Turner's innovations of colour and tone, and his increasingly interpretative rather than repetitive attitude to the old masters had already earned him attacks as the underminer of the moral and aesthetic integrity of his art, in terms which, as one observer remarked, were usually 'reserved for *crime*'; he threatened his fellow painters with a contagion, an 'Influenza in Art'. Byron's first offering, *Hours of Idleness* – while avowedly the work of a 'minor' – had been accused by the *Edinburgh Review* of irreverence, of aspiring to 'the class which neither Gods nor Men are said to permit'. In future years this vein of criticism was to be tapped more deeply and damningly, above all by Southey, one of the Lake Poets Byron came to abhor, in the preface to his *Vision of Judgment* of 1821. By then – that is, after the publication of the 'lascivious' *Don Juan* the previous year – Byron had confirmed himself as dangerously immoral and corrupting of moral values, the perpetrator of Constable's 'deadly slime'.

But in *English Bards and Scotch Reviewers*, Byron had served notice that he would give as good as he got. Assuming Pope's mantle, he rounded on his early critics in a parody of their own attacks, grafting his vengeful satire on the 'Scotch Reviewers' to a mockery of the 'English Bards' – chiefly the newly fashionable Lake Poets – that he had meditated as early as 1807. It was a witty notion, deliberately self-promoting and bound, for better or worse, to isolate him from his peers; and it could well have brought him to Turner's special attention, for in tone and sentiment it chimed with much of Turner's thinking at the time. It even included a generous tribute to Turner's fellow painter Martin Archer Shee, whose *Rhymes on Art*, first published in 1805 and expanded as *Elements of Art* in 1809, did much to stimulate Turner's poetic efforts:

And here let Shee and Genius find a place,
Whose pen and pencil yield an equal grace;
To guide whose hand the sister arts combine
And trace the poet's or the painter's line;
Whose magic touch can bid the canvas glow,
Or pour the easy rhyme's harmonious flow.

Shee's poem, subtitled 'The Remonstrance of a Painter', may indeed be numbered as an ancestor of Byron's more pointed satire. Couched in Augustan couplets, it attacked the established art world of London with its sub-standard painters and prejudiced or complacent critics, contrasted the prevailing gloom with Britain's high reputation in the other liberal arts, and, more constructively, pleaded for judicious patronage and proper access to great works of art. These issues were to ferment for a number of years, but were of special concern to Turner, with his high sense of destiny and pride in his nationhood, in a period when he was coming under attack from lesser minds. Like Byron, he responded to criticism by attacking not only his critics, but also the incompetents and hacks they saw fit to admire.

Turner's early poetic concerns and ambitions have been thoroughly investigated by Andrew Wilton and need no fresh discussion here. But it should be remembered that among them was a keen preoccupation with ineptitude and failed inspiration both in poetry – the sister art he so greatly loved but in which he recognised his own inadequacy – and in painting. About 1808 he made two drawings on the theme of barren creativity, one of an amateur painter gloating over a derivative canvas in a studio scattered with old masters to work from, and another of a poet struggling for inspiration in a garret; both were elaborated with verses (figs.1, 2). The study of the poet was adopted for the painting, 'The Garreteer's Petition', shown at the Royal Academy in 1809 (no.6). That this painting should appear two months after the publication of Byron's excoriating attack on literary incompetence, and in the very same month as it went into a sec-

left
fig.1 'The Garreteer's Petition', *c.*1808, pen and brown ink and wash with some watercolour. *Tate Gallery* (D08256)
right
fig.2 'The Artist's Studio', *c.*1808, pen and brown ink and wash with some watercolour and scraping out. *Tate Gallery* (D08257)

ond edition to meet popular demand, seems an extraordinary coincidence, to say the least. One is tempted to see a precise connection between Turner's picture, with its ironic print of Mount Parnassus on the wall in the background, and the poem that Byron's friend Dallas had wanted called 'The Parish Poor of Parnassus'; and one wonders what Byron might have made of it had he strayed into the Academy in the last weeks before his departure abroad.

Connections of this kind remain elusive, but it is certainly true that Turner and Byron had been roused to their rebarbative mood by the same critical climate – and by some of the same people. The identity of the smug amateur of painting in Turner's drawing has been much discussed, but there is one candidate who would perfectly fit the bill – Sir George Beaumont. That talented painter and influential connoisseur was famous for his borrowings from the old masters and his suspicion of any vigorous manifestations of originality. For several years he had been the most aggressive of Turner's critics, taking a tone that implied that nothing short of moral values was at stake; and these strictures, coupled with his no less vigorous promotion of the young painter David Wilkie, were earning him a good deal of resentment from artists who fell between these two extremes and so tended to be ignored by him. Nor was Beaumont only 'Supreme Dictator of works of art' or 'the Demagogue of the picture Criticks', as two painters called him; he was also, with his wife, far the most fashionable patron of modern poets – and exactly those poets who left Byron cold. Had Turner and Byron met about 1809, they would surely have made common cause over Beaumont at least – that self-proclaimed man of taste who saw nothing in one of them, and everything in those colleagues the other most despised.

If Beaumont needed any encouragement, it had been the poet and dramatist William Sotheby – who in fact was thrown a crumb of praise in *English Bards* – who in 1801 challenged him to take up the cudgels on behalf of British art. Dedicating to Beaumont a *Poetical Epistle on the Encouragement of the British School of Painting*, he urged his patron to 'invoke the senate! bid the nation hear!' – thus anticipating Shee's pleas four years later. It was Sotheby too who opened the Beaumonts' eyes to modern poetry by introducing them to Coleridge. Wordsworth was admitted to their charmed circle, and Southey followed soon afterwards, while yet another pet aversion of Byron's, the Revd William Lisle Bowles, bibulous editor and undistinguished sonneteer, clung on to the periphery, good for some lines on Beaumont's latest Rubens or Wilkie; Byron gave Bowles short shrift in *English Bards*, offended as he was by Bowles's officious and censorious edition of Pope, published in 1806, in which the editor had cast gratuitous aspersions on Pope's moral character.

The Beaumonts' greatest love, as is well known, was Wordsworth. With him they enjoyed a friendship deep and passionate, and fuelled by a certain amount of overheated sentiment, that lasted the rest of their lives; they showed, besides, extraordinary tolerance of Coleridge's aberrations. 'The most sensible and pleasing man I ever knew' was the verdict on Beaumont given by Walter Scott, another friend, and there is no doubt that he was a sensitive and appreciative critic. But, with the exception of Coleridge, the Beaumonts' circle of poets was made up of men who knew their place – an attribute hardly to be expected of Byron whose intellect Lady Beaumont deemed 'near derangement' in 1815 when, having come to terms with some 'wild and beautiful flowers of poetry' in *The Giaour* and *The Corsair,* she entertained him with Scott and Rogers. In 1812 she had more rashly invited him with Wordsworth, but, not surprisingly, no friendship ensued, and in 1823 Byron decided to publish his 'literary eclogue', *The Blues,* written three years earlier, in which he poked wicked fun at what he saw as the Beaumonts' intellectual pretensions and breathless lion-hunting, casting them as Sir George and Lady Bluemount; their friends 'Mouthy', 'Wordswords' and 'Scamp' (Coleridge), 'those of the lake', suffered another panning here, and Sotheby too was damned by association, featuring as Botherby, a flatulent creep.[6]

Byron later recanted some of the abuse thrown so freely in *English Bards,* explaining to Coleridge that it had been written 'while very young, and very angry', and for a time – but only for a time – mending relations with Southey. Yet it may well have been as a figure of controversy, as the butt of a particular strain of criticism who was prepared to hit back in kind, that Byron first impressed himself upon Turner as he did on many others. But the question remains; when did Turner begin to read Byron seriously, in such a way as to sense affinities with his own art and mind? *Childe Harold* was always the poem, and Byron the solitary, meditative, impressionable traveller, that affected him most, but how soon did he read it, and form a picture of its author?

TURNER AND 'CHILDE HAROLD'S PILGRIMAGE'

The first concrete evidence of Turner reading anything from *Childe Harold* comes from 1817. Visiting the Low Countries, the Rhineland and the battlefield of Waterloo, he took with him a guidebook by Charles Campbell, freshly issued in a second edition and quoting, at the appropriate spot, Byron's memorable lines on Waterloo from the third canto of *Childe Harold* published the previous year – lines which Turner could also have read reprinted in the *Times.* Turner's 'Field of Waterloo', exhibited in 1818 (no.35), was manifestly affected by Byron's grim picture of the aftermath of battle, and was indeed the first picture he showed with a quotation from the poet. But the third canto was not published until 1816, to rather more muted praise than its two predecessors which had run through ten editions by 1815. If Turner's future friend George Jones could begin a set of illustrations to *Childe Harold* as early as 1812, it seems inconceivable that Turner had not already come across it, or at the very least some of its most important reviews – for example those (both unsigned) by Jeffrey in the *Edinburgh Review* or George Ellis in the *Quarterly* that greeted the first cantos in May 1812. Even if he did not see them in London, perhaps he was able to read them at Farnley Hall in November that year, for as a miscellaneous writer himself, his host Walter Fawkes must have kept his library well stocked with the latest books and journals.

It was perhaps Fawkes who did more than anyone to nurture Turner's interest in Byron, and foster sentiments that he could recognise in his poetry. The Fawkes family was keen on poetry, and it is easy to see that Byron would have made a special appeal to a man of Fawkes's sensibilities. In 1810 Fawkes published a *Chronology of the History of Modern Europe*, so he would have been acutely aware of the historical allusions in *Childe Harold*; moreover he had prefaced the book with a proto-Byronic quotation from Young's *Night Thoughts*, in which the ghosts of history are summoned as ironic commentators on human achievements and the ravages of time. Turner's copy, presented to him by Fawkes (no.30), would have prepared him for such sentiments in Byron. Fawkes's blend of patrician liberalism, with its emphasis on individual freedoms, was also such as to render him sensitive to Byron's frequent animadversions on lost liberty in Greece or Italy. Later Fawkes was to commission Turner's first direct illustration to Byron in watercolour, a view of the Athenian Acropolis inscribed with a reduction of the famous line from *The Giaour*, 'T'is living Greece no more' (p.97) and he also acquired a watercolour of the dehumanising carnage at Waterloo (fig.3) that carried the spirit of Byron's lines at least as powerfully as the larger version in oil.

fig.3 'Battle of Waterloo', 1817, watercolour (w 494). *Syndics of the Fitzwilliam Museum, Cambridge*

As a picture of Europe in the shadow of Napoleon, still ravaged by war, *Childe Harold* was outstanding from the first. If we doubt Turner's capacity to appreciate its didactic, reflective and philosophical dimensions, its many allusive digressions, we need only consider one of his own recent poetic efforts – a long poem to accompany and knit together the drawings he had begun in the summer of 1811 on a tour of the south coast of England.[7] The tour was hardly to be compared to Byron's epic travels – Byron was by this time in Greece – and the verses are so awkward as to be unpublishable. But the idea may legitimately be compared to Byron's, and shared a similar Augustan ancestry. Turner also had been sketching an extended topographical epic, meditating along the way upon history, industry, nature and science. Stirring in his imagination was an English *Childe Harold* – without the Childe. Byron's poem could almost have been written for Turner, and when years later he came to illustrate places described in it or connected with its composition, it was with the experience – however tortured – of having attempted to weave a connecting poetic thread between his own discrete observations of place. To be able thus to reverse the process was a unique qualification; Turner alone could supply for Byron the sort of separate images he had struggled to link poetically himself.

The scope of Byron's travels, as revealed in *Childe Harold,* was remarkable for the period. It is often said of Turner that he was unable to travel abroad until after the Napoleonic War, but in the first two cantos Byron proved it *was* possible – Britain, after all, controlled the seas – and must have sharpened Turner's appetite for new horizons. Byron had considered a visit to Germany, Austria and St Petersburg in 1806, and it had been lack of money as much as politics that had kept him at home; a plan to sail to the Hebrides and Iceland in 1807 also failed, as did a more ambitious trip the following year to 'the Mediterranean, or to the West Indies, or – to the devil'. Byron's frustrated wanderlust in these years impressed itself strongly on the portraitist and miniaturist George Sanders, who in 1807 began the remarkable portrait of the poet and a page with a sailing boat on some wild shore (no.1). With a flash of extraordinary prescience, this usually mediocre painter conjured up both the author and the hero of *Childe Harold,* before a word of it was written. It was only in 1809 that Byron put his travel plans into effect, going by sea to Portugal and Spain, and then to the Eastern Mediterranean, to Albania and Greece. He had fantasised about continuing to India and Persia, but even without these exotic destinations his tour was a fascinating blend of the familiar and the unexplored, the accessible and the remote.

As material for a picturesque epic, Byron's itinerary varied in originality. There were few poems or literary sources on Spain and Portugal, rather more on Greece, where Byron found himself drawn into a wide and mixed circle of Europeans, and none on Albania, then hardly visited at all. For his part, Turner was probably most interested in the Greek passages of *Childe Harold.* As he read Byron's strictures on Lord Elgin and his appropriation of the marbles, and his notes on Elgin's agent and draughtsman G.B. Lusieri, he would have recalled that he himself had been offered the very same job in 1799; had Turner gone to Greece with Elgin, and found himself as busy as Lusieri did, it might even have been he who was there to accompany Byron on his visits to sites like Cape Colonna. Unlike Byron, Turner wholeheartedly approved of the Elgin marbles being brought to London, where they could nourish the interest in classical Greece that inspired a number of his important early pictures. But Byron's poetry also moved the reader to a consideration of modern Greece, and to a critical comparison of past and present. Inevitably poignant in the cases of Greece and Italy that were then under unsympathetic foreign domination, such comparisons are a recurrent theme of *Childe Harold,* and Turner's response to the poem, at least on canvas, drew heavily on them.

But they are also part of the Augustan heritage the two men shared, and, ironically enough, it was Southey rather than Byron who provided the precise literary spur to the two Greek pictures that were Turner's first pairing of ancient and modern (figs.4, 5), the views of the temple at Aegina of which Gally Knight had given him his sketch (see no.26). Yet despite the appearance of Southey's lines, from his *Roderick, the Last of the Goths*, in the

fig.4 'Temple of Jupiter Panellenius Restored', exh. 1816, oil on canvas (B&J 133). *Richard L. Feigen, New York*

fig.5 'View of the Temple of Jupiter Panellenius, in the island of Aegina, with the Greek National Dance of the Romaika: the Acropolis of Athens in the Distance. Painted from a sketch by H. Gally Knight, Esq. in 1810', exh.1816, oil on canvas (B&J 134). *The Duke of Northumberland, K.G.*

fig.6 Thomas Phillips, 'Portrait of Byron in Albanian Dress', 1813, oil on canvas. *National Portrait Gallery, London*

Academy catalogue alongside Turner's view of the restored temple, these are the first paintings in which we may detect what was later to become an overtly Byronic spirit.[8]

Two years earlier, in 1814, if Turner read Hazlitt's qualified praise of his classical 'Dido and Aeneas' (Tate Gallery; B&J 129) in the *Morning Chronicle*, he would also have seen his warm remarks on Thomas Phillips's 'Portrait of a Nobleman in Albanian Dress', a version of the famous portrait of Byron in Arnout costume (fig.6); perhaps by then he was in a position to agree with Hazlitt's verdict that it 'conveys the softness and wildness of character of the popular poet of the East'. Phillips's portrait defined a prevailing concept of Byron, and its somewhat affected anonymity was calculated to foster the tantalising association between Byron and the Byronic hero. The same year, Richard Westall's no less striking portrait – brooding and intense whereas Phillips's was haughty – appeared in the artist's one-man show in Pall Mall; Westall had already spoken to Joseph Farington 'of Lord Byron whose portrait is a very singular character'. Byron's public image, compounded of stories and scandals of his private life, the recollection of his foreign travel and the misanthropic musings of his creations, was a matter of admiration and speculation. Before long, its increasingly Mephistophelian tinge would arouse open disgust. It was impossible to separate the man and his work, and Scott, reviewing the third canto of *Childe Harold* and *The Prisoner of Chillon* in the *Quarterly* in October 1817, asked the question on everyone's lips; was the evil and guilt of Byron's heroes truly the poet's own, and why? Scott could not provide an answer, but it was the poet's character and experiences, as much as his work, that propelled him into the arena of art. In Rome in 1828, Turner was able to see his friend Charles Eastlake complete one of the most important of all renderings of Byron the melancholy traveller in distant lands – by then the least contentious definition of the poet. Ostensibly an illustration but manifestly a picture of the poet himself, 'Lord Byron's "Dream"' (no.19) was based on the poem that Moore was to describe as 'the most mournful, as well as picturesque "story of a wandering life" that ever came from the pen and heart of man'. Although Eastlake seems to have taken his composition from Turner's view of the ruined temple at Aegina, he could enter more completely than most into his subject, for he too had been in Greece, in 1818, and had met many of Byron's old contacts in Athens, including Lusieri. After Fawkes, Eastlake was certainly the keenest Byronist among Turner's close friends, and in 1830 he was to linger longer in the poet's footsteps, taking his old apartment in the Palazzo Mocenigo in Venice (no.9) for two months in the summer. Meanwhile, his picture, exhibited in London in 1829, stood as a memorial to the early Byron, the Byron of *Childe Harold*, and surely the Byron to whom Turner responded most warmly; indeed a year later Turner would begin the serious work of illustrating his 'wandering life'.

Definitive as his picture was, Eastlake had taken but one image from a sequence in a poem expressing the pangs of doomed love. *The Dream* had been written in Switzerland in 1816, in bitterness after the failure of Byron's marriage and his final departure for Continental exile. 1816 was truly a turning point, both in Byron's personal fortunes and in his literary standing. The third canto of *Childe Harold* proved as commercially popular as its predecessors when it appeared that year – Murray sold 7000 copies at a booksellers' dinner in December – but its more openly unorthodox tone drew reservations even from Byron's friends. Byron had written it spasmodically as he travelled through Belgium, the Rhineland and Switzerland. The Waterloo stanzas, soon to accompany Turner on his own visit to the battlefield, were written after Byron had trodden the ground and gathered relics both gruesome and touching, and the companionship of Shelley, his devoted admirer and his neighbour that summer by the lake at Geneva, had encouraged pantheistic meditations 'In solitude, where we are least alone'. Gibbon, Voltaire and Rousseau were acknowledged as spirits of the place, while the place itself was given a new dominance and – with its thunders and splashings of rain, the grasshopper's 'good-night carol' or the 'floating whisper' of the hills – a voice of its own. Byron was soon accused of purloining Wordsworth's treatment of nature, and indeed his assertion

> I live not in myself, but I become
> Portion of that around me: and to me
> High mountains are a feeling

steered too close to plagiarism for comfort, not least because it was less than convincing; one modern critic[9] has delivered an outright 'No!' to Byron's question

> Are not the mountains, waves, and skies, a part
> Of me and of my soul, as I of them?
> Is not the love of these deep in my heart
> With a pure passion?

Yet it is hard not to be moved by these lines. They speak for an age if not truly for their author, and one can imagine Turner, who according to Ruskin treasured Byron as a poet of nature, responding with a triumphant affirmative.

The third canto revealed other and more genuine facets of Byron's latest cast of mind that were to be developed further, and offend more harshly. Shelley, that confirmed atheist who shared Byron's impatience with the hypocrisies of conventional morality, had not only encouraged Byron's metaphysical interests, but stoked his incipient radicalism. Cast out of England and rejected by a smug and complacent society to which he had only ever belonged superficially, Byron now turned to the oppressed, defeated or demoralised peoples of Europe with an open heart, and with a wistful longing for their lost freedoms. His stanzas on Waterloo declared his refusal to glory in Napoleon's defeat and rather his feeling for the common dead, while his active sympathy for the fallen Emperor (whose exile was all too like his own) had also been apparent in four political poems, supposedly translations 'From the French', included in a small volume Murray brought out just six weeks after Byron left England. The *Champion* had already attacked one of these for its evident lack of patriotism, and even Scott, generally so sympathetic, was later to condemn Byron's even-handedness when writing of Waterloo. Meanwhile he advised Byron to 'submit' to the disciplines of religion and philosophy.

In so far as his critics sensed new tendencies in Byron's thought, *Childe Harold* III was less liked than the earlier cantos. Indeed, Turner took something of a risk in adopting Byron's vision of Waterloo for his own (no.35). Otherwise he must have enjoyed this canto for its vivid and moving evocations of scenery he remembered from his first Swiss tour in 1802, and its comprehensive references to the memories and associations of the European landscape; and perhaps the same connection was made by Fawkes, who had acquired most of the finished watercolours based on

Turner's 1802 tour. Possibly also it was Fawkes who encouraged Turner to take a hint from Byron, and follow in the poet's footsteps from Belgium along the Rhine in 1817; once again, Fawkes bought the resulting water-colours, including one of the dead at Waterloo. Although the Rhine, with its majestic scenery and rich history, was sufficiently interesting for itself and already the subject of travel literature (no.32), Turner's decision to make it the object of his first Continental tour so soon after *Childe Harold* III has generally been thought more than mere coincidence, and as with his Swiss work, his drawings and Byron's poetry would work in counterpoint.

While Turner drew the Rhine, Byron was in Venice, at work on *Childe Harold* IV. Devoted to Italy, it was published in 1818, to a mixed reception. Some reviewers found their response shaded by prurient interest in the rumours of Byron's profligate life in Venice; others found fault with the structure of the poem. Moore once reported that Lord William Russell had heard that Byron had at first been unmoved by Rome and at a loss what to write about, until his friend J.C. Hobhouse 'gave him the heads of what he afterwards described so powerfully'. For Hazlitt, the resulting travel-ogue was an unhappy concept; he found it difficult to sustain his interest or to see the relevance of the 'accidental occurence of different objects – the Venus of Medici, – or the Statue of Pompey, – the Capitol at Rome, or the Bridge of Sighs at Venice'.[10] But if Turner were already dreaming of a visit to Italy, there could have been no greater encouragement than this canto with its hymn to the beauties of the 'Mother of Arts! as once of Arms' and its melancholy reflections on fallen greatness. Byron's vision of Italy as a land of decaying splendour and ghostly heroes, finally redeemed by the loveliness of nature, was soon to be Turner's own, and the fourth canto was to be the most fruitful source for quotations to apply to his own pictures.

Hazlitt had followed his strictures on *Childe Harold* IV with the hope that some 'Historical Illustrations' being prepared by Hobhouse would eluci-date the poet's purpose. Byron's companion on his first tour abroad, at Geneva in 1816 and afterwards from time to time in Italy, Hobhouse was also a sound scholar, well fitted to write such an accompaniment. He had begun it in Venice, where he could use the Ducal library, and the work grew to such a size that it had finally to be issued in two parts, the first attached to an edition of *Childe Harold* IV itself, the second in a separate volume. Byron dedicated the canto to him and his *Illustrations* were a sub-stantial amplification of the text, providing a wealth of antiquarian and literary information. They were the first important example of the various companions to Byron, both literary and artistic, that became a veritable industry after the poet's death.

The richness of reference in *Childe Harold* and in other poems of Byron clearly called for further exposition. Hobhouse's approach was essentially to produce extended footnotes, but to the engraver, William Finden,

Byron's work cried out for topographical illustration. Its magnificently varied landscape settings were gifts to the illustrator. Thus it was that in 1830 Turner was commissioned by Finden – who soon secured the collaboration of Murray – to produce a series of realisations of Byronic landscape, showing the settings of the poetry and places connected with the author; and as we shall see, Hobhouse himself played a large and ultimately very damaging part in the enterprise. Finden's *Landscape Illustrations* to Byron appeared between 1832 and 1834, published by Murray, and meanwhile Turner had also been retained to provide vignette landscapes for a popular edition of Murray's, bringing together Moore's standard life of Byron, first published in 1830, and the poet's complete works. Both projects are described later in this essay.

While reserving the freedom to write on Byron himself, Hobhouse had been distinctly obstructive to Moore as he was to all who attempted to publish on his old friend. He was obsessively jealous of the wealth of personal information he had accumulated and had since retained as Byron's executor, and understandably suspicious of anything that might add to the rather dubious mythology that surrounded Byron's memory. His guardianship became more cautious as Byron's reputation fell, and he had in any case disapproved of much of his later work, actually advising him to suppress *Don Juan* (1819). He had not been alone in finding 'licentiousness' and 'downright indecency' in the later Byron, for the poet's searches for a new direction in his writing through a bolder assertion of personal and moral freedom and a more open critique of conventional doctrine had proved widely contentious. Even his old friends and Murray's Albemarle Street 'Synod' had worried at the pervasive scepticism and irreverence of Byron's last works, and *Don Juan* caused complete uproar, striking many as the work of a truly Satanic mind. In April 1823, a year before his death, Byron had written to Moore that he was as 'low in popularity and book-selling as any writer can be'.

In fact this was untrue. However much his enemies attacked him or his friends squirmed, Byron's appeal to the general reader remained as high as ever, sustained by his earlier work. Murray printed edition after edition to satisfy demand, and the industry was given fresh impetus by the poet's death. Dying so young, in the cause of Greek independence, added a martyr's palm to Byron's poetic laurels. Turner was almost alone among his contemporaries, from the greatest to the humblest, in neither remarking the event nor recording what he was doing when he heard the news. But two years earlier he had joined with the Fawkes family in making his own modest tribute to Byron and his commitment to Greece. For a compilation for the Farnley library of works by Byron, Scott and Moore, he had drawn a frontispiece, 'Three Poets in Three Kingdoms Born', and contributed his illustration to *The Giaour*. He had already shown his 'Field of Waterloo', (no.35) with its quotation from *Childe Harold*, at the Academy

in 1818, and the same year Murray began to publish James Hakewill's *Picturesque Tour in Italy* with his illustrations, one of which, 'The Cascade of
Terni' (no.33), appeared near Hakewill's quotation from 'a great modern
poet'. The poet of course was Byron, and the lines came from *Childe
Harold*. Now, Turner's drawings for Fawkes marked further steps in the
voyage into Byron that would yield its richest results in the years after the
poet's death.

'MODERN THOUGHT': TURNER'S BYRONIC
PAINTINGS AND THEIR BACKGROUND

In 1813 the young C.R. Leslie, in London to win his spurs as a painter,
had written home to his sister in America, 'pictures from modern poets do
not take'. Even such poetic icons as Shakespeare, Milton and Dante
seemed to him 'scarcely sufficiently canonised to be firm ground'. Leslie's
judgement needs qualification, not least because he was to make such a
lucrative career as a painter of literature. In fact, within twenty years modern British poets, led by Byron, were to become highly fertile sources for
painters and illustrators at home and abroad, while it was the old masters
of poetry whose popularity relatively declined. They did not disappear, but
tended to be rendered more often within the small compass of engravings
in popular reprints, than on the extended canvas of such paintings as had
appeared not long before in Boydell's Shakespeare Gallery or Fuseli's
Milton Gallery. As the fashion for monumental history painting declined,
artists began to change alliegance to the new stars of contemporary literature, to Byron, Scott and Moore; and to seek a new pictorial vocabulary
outside the language of the Grand Style.

It was in 1814 that the first Byron subjects appeared at the Royal
Academy. The painters were popular historical and literary illustrators,
Henry Singleton and Richard Corbould, and their subjects were from *The
Corsair*, just published. This poem seems to have had an immediate visual
appeal, and remained for many years among the most painted and illustrated of Byron's poems. The same year, the Princess of Wales asked Fuseli
to paint a subject from Byron, and he chose the same theme from the
poem as Singleton had done, 'Conrad Freeing Gulnare' (no.15). This was
exactly the sort of Byron subject – intensely dramatic, exotic and exuding
romantic interest – that caught the popular imagination and would recur
in countless images from the inspired masterpieces of Delacroix to the
humblest vignettes of the keepsake engravers. Along with *The Corsair*, it was
the Oriental tales, *The Bride of Abydos* and *The Giaour*, that proved the most
enduringly appealing to artists. *Childe Harold*, despite its phenomenal
success, was assimilated less quickly, presumably because its narrative was

less dramatic and its hero a more complex case whose condition could only be understood through his reflections on the landscape through which he travelled.

George Jones began a series of drawings of the Childe's adventures (nos.10–12) in 1812, before turning to *The Giaour* the following year (nos.13, 14), but his figure subjects scarcely do justice to the poem and never appeared publicly in any form. They are however of great interest in being among the earliest, if not in fact the very first, illustrations to the poem by a British artist. At the Academy, the first *Childe Harold* subjects were shown in 1817. The artist was one J.R. Walker, and his offerings were presumably both landscapes, one being 'Monastic Zitza' from the second canto and the other, unspecified, coming from the third canto. Neither of these can have hinted at the riches Turner was to draw from the poem. In his own paintings and drawings, he revealed a reading that was less specific and episodic, but often more thoughtful and comprehensive, than that of even his greatest contemporaries.

As we have seen, it was in 1818 that Turner first quoted from *Childe Harold* in a Royal Academy catalogue, appending stanzas from the third canto to his 'Field of Waterloo' (no.35). It was a fitting beginning to his public association with Byron, for post-Napoleonic Europe, whose future had been decided on that fateful field, was to be the domain in which he looked to Byron to support and enhance his work. If there was a long gap between this painting and his next Byronic exhibit, the Italian landscape entitled simply 'Childe Harold's Pilgrimage – Italy' (no.36) shown in 1832, it was surely because Turner needed to understand both his subject and the poet better, for only when he relt ready to offer a definitive statement of his chosen theme did he turn to Byron for his text. Thereafter there were to be only four more Byron pictures, a Rhine subject (p.93), a splendid conspectus of 'Modern Rome' (no.37) and views of Venice from near and afar (nos.38, 39), exhibited between 1835 and 1844.

It is hardly surprising that Turner developed his response to Byron in the second half of his career. Now a restless traveller himself, with all Byron's receptiveness to the echoes of history, he must often have been reminded of the poet as he trod in the Childe's footsteps. It was only natural, perhaps, to acknowledge by a judicious quotation the connections that would have struck most Academy visitors. But was Turner doing more than recognising an elective affinity? How far was his vision of continental Europe actually formed by Byron's? Certainly he seems to have gone out of his way to emphasise a special relationship with the poet. Although he had availed himself of the opportunity to accompany his pictures with quotations ever since the Academy first permitted it, in 1798, no other modern poet was included by his own name and that of one of his works in their actual titles. Yet not all of Turner's Byron pictures can in any material sense be said to be illustrations of the chosen texts. What of the others? Either Turner simply tacked on a few appropriate lines from a now familiar and favourite poet, or he had so far absorbed the Byronic spirit that it permeated his whole vision, enabling the image to comprehend more of Byron than just a few words.

How highly we estimate Byron's influence over Turner must depend on our estimate of Byron himself, for if he merely summarised the experiences and attitudes of an age, it was only to be expected that Turner would have shared them. But such an idea scarcely does justice to poet or painter. Byron's destiny was to lead rather than to follow, and Turner, who took it for granted that poets should be prophets, would have expected no less. The European itineraries Turner shared with Byron were common enough at the time; he did not need Byron to conduct him to Waterloo – which had been trampled by hordes of tourists since the summer of 1815 – or the Rhineland, and least of all to Italy. But in the Academy in 1818, it would have been clear to all, and shocking to many, that Turner had read and *felt* the lines he quoted alongside his 'Field of Waterloo'. Image and word were not always to be so precisely matched in his subsequent Byronic pictures, but nor were they casually conjoined.

Turner's 'Waterloo' ran absolutely counter to the established tradition of the victorious battle picture; it was, for example, the last thing the British Institution had in mind when in 1816 it offered a premium of one thousand guineas for a large sketch of the recent triumph. It does not even depict the battle at all, but the carnage left behind afterwards. No glorious heroism or tactical genius is celebrated, nor is there any distinction between opposing sides, but only the dead among whom friend and foe, officers, men and horses are jumbled regardless. To a London audience, few of whom had actually seen a battle, it must have been an extraordinary revelation, hardly to be matched before Roger Fenton's photographs arrived from the Crimea. But unlike those, it was a feat of the imagination. Turner had done his research, walking over the field and noting the numbers killed in particular places; there were guides aplenty to point out the grim statistics, and accounts of the events after the battle – the thunderstorm, the looting and the poignant search for personal remains – were now available. But Turner's conception is nevertheless remarkable. It is also very precisely Byron's, and Turner's quotation from *Childe Harold* made the connection explicit for his audience. Campbell's guide, which Turner had taken with him to Waterloo, quoted more conventionally celebratory verses by Scott and Southey as well as Byron, but Turner chose Byron's memorable account of the fateful progress from ballroom to battlefield and then to death 'in one red burial blent'. Such a relentlessly grim image for a glorious victory and the fall of a hostile empire was perfectly tuned to Turner's own sense of the ultimate futility of human endeavour – that pervasive and melancholy idea that had already produced his great parable of an ancient empire-builder on the way to his doom, 'Hannibal

Crossing the Alps' (Tate Gallery; B&J 126), and was emerging in his own occasional verses, *The Fallacies of Hope*.

Nor would Turner have missed Byron's image of man returning to nature – the earth 'cover'd thick with other clay, /which her own clay shall cover'. Across the wide philosophical and historical perspectives that came naturally to Turner's mind, individual achievements, partial loyalties, paled into insignificance beside the eternal problem of man's place in the natural world. Guided by Byron, Turner saw that it was not possible to celebrate even such an apocalyptic event as Waterloo either in isolation, or with unequivocal enthusiasm. Nor could he take only a nationalist or patriotic side; impossible to forget that in that beginning was also an ending, and in that victory, defeat. As Byron had warned in an earlier stanza, 'Stop! – for thy tread is on an Empire's dust!' In the poem, Byron is able to look forward. Childe Harold stands on the field a year after the battle and observes 'How that red rain hath made the harvest grow!' Turner has fixed a vision of utter desolation, the Romantic equivalent of the nuclear night – just as Byron did so terrifyingly in another poem, *Darkness* – that men might learn of the horrors of war and the folly of ambition. But his picture, like Byron's verses in *Childe Harold*, had a more popular appeal; through it, comrades and widows could grieve and lament.

In Byron's case, however, refraining from vainglorious rejoicing was taken by conservative critics more in a political than a moral context. The poet asked his readers to '*prove* before ye praise' and displayed an unhealthy scepticism as to the motives of the victors and the prospects for the Europe they had created:

> but is Earth more free?
> Did nations combat to make One submit;
> Or league to teach all kings true sovereignty?
> What! shall reviving Thraldom again be
> The patch'd up idol of enlighten'd days?

Though he thought it affected, and not to be taken too seriously, Scott censured Byron's evident liberalism in a retrospective review – occasioned mainly by *Childe Harold* IV – that appeared in the same year as Turner's 'Waterloo'. To refer, as Byron did in dedicating the completed poem to Hobhouse, to Waterloo as 'the carnage of Mont St. Jean' seemed to Scott a disgraceful aberration; he objected also to Byron's 'disdainful denunciations' of his own country.[11] But Byron did not always please the radicals either. Hazlitt, who had stalked London unshaven and wearing a black armband in the days after the battle, found Byron's passages on Bonaparte insincere in that they first compared him to the heroes of antiquity, and then criticised him; Hazlitt continued (in an attack the poet bitterly resented) as if to accuse Byron himself of falling into the same errors as the Emperor:

why then should Lord Byron force the comparison between the modern and the ancient hero? It is because the slaves of power mind the cause they have to serve, because their own interest is incurred; but the friends of liberty always sacrifice their cause, which is *only* the cause of humanity, to their own spleen, vanity, and self- opinion. The league between tyrants and slaves is a chain of adamant; the bond between poets and people is a rope of sand.[12]

Whether Turner's picture became tarred with the same liberal or unpatriotic brush as the verses that had helped to inspire it is not directly evident from its reviews; they do not admit a political dimension in so many words, although such comparisons as that in the *Annals of the Fine Arts* to 'a drunken hubbub on an illumination night' may reveal the critic's inclination to laugh at something that made him uneasy. Significantly, however, it was Hazlitt's *Examiner* that gave the most generous review, acknowledging a genuine humanity in Turner's conception that it had missed in Byron's. It was Turner, without Byron's aristocratic aloofness and political disaffection, who had found the true common touch as he painted 'the wives and brothers and sons of the slain come, with anxious eyes and agonised hearts, to look at Ambition's charnel house after the slaughtered victims of legitimate selfishness and wickedness'.

It was not until 1832 that Turner again referred to Byron in a painting. 'Childe Harold's Pilgrimage – Italy' (no.36) was a magnificent celebration of the land both poet and painter had come to love, and of the poem that best expressed the painter's own feelings about it. Perhaps Turner called it to mind in Rome in 1828, as he watched his friend Eastlake at work on his painting 'Lord Byron's "Dream"' (no.19) – surely the most ambitious attempt to date to reconcile the Byronic hero and his landscape – and for the past two years he had been engaged in making watercolour illustrations to *Childe Harold* for Murray and the Findens (nos.46–83). Now he felt ready to blend his mature understanding of the poem with a synoptic rendering of the beauties of Italy. The painting is a conspectus of many things characteristically Italian – the Tiber, the Campagna, the bridges at Narni, the Temple of Clitumnus, the vistas from Tivoli – pervaded by an air of exquisite decay. For it Turner chose lines from *Childe Harold* IV:

> – and now, fair Italy!
> Thou art the garden of the world.
> Even in thy desert what is like to thee?
> Thy very weeds are beautiful, thy waste
> More rich than other climes' fertility:
> Thy wreck a glory, and thy ruin graced
> With an immaculate charm which cannot be defaced.

The painting's title asserts that it is Turner's key Byronic statement to date

– and it was never superseded as such – but its relationship to the poem has troubled critics; of all his Byronic pictures, it has seemed to epitomise an understanding of the poet either imperfect or superficial. Robert Altick has spoken for many commentators in finding the picture typical of Turner's approach in making only a 'glancing reference' to *Childe Harold*;[13] and indeed a surface reading suggests that Turner took as much from the paintings of Claude as from Byron's poem. A more fruitful interpretation is Ruskin's, but even this fails because it does not fully acknowledge the simple fact that Turner was painting not Childe Harold himself – neither his specific adventures nor his character and moral stance (which indeed Byron himself often forgot in the poem) – but the Childe's Italy, which was now also his own.

Ruskin thought very highly of this picture. It was for him 'the loveliest work of the second period', and one which exemplified Turner's engage-ment in 'modern thought'. Remarking on Turner's profound debt to literature, Ruskin traced a progress from 'the influence of classic writers only' – Virgil and Ovid in Italian subjects, the Augustans Thomson and Pope in English ones – to a predominant concern with contemporaries, beginning with Rogers and proceeding to Scott and Byron. Ruskin con-nected Turner's discovery of Byron with the calmer, more contemplative love of nature that comes with maturity, and found both beautifully ex-pressed in 'Italy'. He thought the extract Turner chose from *Childe Harold* 'truly describes the general motives of the picture', but also recognised its description of a larger state of mind:

> the richest and sweetest passages of Byron, which usually address
> themselves most to the imagination of youth, became an inspiration
> to Turner in his later years; and an inspiration so compelling, that,
> while he only illustrated here and there a detached passage from other
> poets, he endeavoured as far as in him lay, to delineate the whole
> mind of Byron. He fastened on incidents related in the other poems;
> this is the only picture he ever painted to illustrate the poet's own
> mind and pilgrimage.

So far so good, but Ruskin went on to find 'the illustration is imperfect, just because it misses the manliest characters of Byron's mind'. Turner should after all have come to Byron younger:

> Turner was fitter to paint Childe Harold when he himself could both
> mock and weep, than now, when he can only dream: and, beautiful as
> the dream may be, he but joins in the injustice too many have done
> to Byron, in dwelling rather on the passionate than the reflective and
> analytic elements of his intellect. ... Turner was strongly influenced,
> from this time forward, by Byron's love of nature; but it is curious
> how unaware he seems of the sterner war of his will and intellect; and

how little this quiet and fair landscape, with its delicate ruin, and softened light, does in reality express the tones of thought into which Harold falls oftenest, in that watchful and weary pilgrimage.[14]

Perhaps Ruskin did not look hard enough. While Turner's purpose was mainly to realise the landscape and condition of the Italy the Childe describes, this infinitely poignant picture also distills his thoughts. We should not expect a literal transcription either of Italy or of the poem, but rather an impression; Turner was operating with the same sweep and selectivity of vision as the poet, as the critic of the *Spectator* realised; 'it is the poetry of art and of nature combined … it bears the same relation to the real scene as does Byron's description'. Yet if we keep in mind the general sense expressed in Turner's quotation from *Childe Harold* – that quintessentially Byronic idea of the peculiar beauty of decay – and proceed to the next few stanzas, we may well feel that Turner has created an account of the poem that is remarkably rich and complete.

Ruskin, while noting the tonal changes that had befallen the picture, nevertheless stressed its 'purple evening light' – a feature now almost completely vanished. The line that immediately followed those quoted was one that Turner afterwards used, and which perfectly matched his own concept of the moon as an image of decay; 'The moon is up, and yet is is not night.' If it were ever there, no moon is visible in the picture today, but a speck of brighter paint in the sky on the right may be 'the single star that reigns with her o'er half the lovely heaven'; and between shadowed foreground and bright horizon, we can indeed see 'Night and Day contending', and the 'paler shadow' that 'strews its mantle o'er the mountains'. Turner has not literally painted Byron's 'deep-dyed Brenta', but his curving river might serve for it; and proceeding further in the poem, we reach Byron's tribute to Petrarch and an evocation of landscape that is perfectly expressed in the picture:

> There is a tomb in Arqua; – rear'd in air
> Pillar'd in their sarcophagus, repose
> The bones of Laura's lover: here repair
> Many familiar with his well-sung woes,
> The pilgrims of his genius. He arose
> To raise a language, and his land reclaim
> From the dull yoke of her barbaric foes:
> Watering the tree which bears his lover's name
> With his melodious tears, he gave himself to fame.

Turner could scarcely have missed this moving tribute from poet to poet. Could not his pillared structure on the distant hill, and the noble tree, have drawn the crowds who have gathered to rest and refresh themselves? Could not the tonsured priest and the girl beside him be suggestive of

Petrarch and Laura themselves? Byron describes Arqua as a mountain village:

> Of that complexion which seems made
> For those who their mortality have felt,
> And sought a refuge from their hopes decay'd
> In the deep umbrage of a green hill's shade,
> Which shows a distant prospect far away
> Of busy cities, now in vain display'd,
> For they can lure no further; and the ray
> Of a bright sun can make sufficient holiday.

Such is the landscape of Turner's picture, and it takes us back to the central image he took from Byron – of an Italy whose loveliness is a consolation for the sorrows of its people, even in its deepest decline. The picture is no less likely to epitomise these lines because it does not precisely describe the Veneto, the Brenta, Arqua or nearby Ferrara; rather Turner has taken this entire section of the poem to represent Italy, and opened out the picture to embrace numerous characteristics of the Italian landscape, just as these stanzas epitomise so much in the larger poem – Byron's description of a land rich in associations, full of echoes of past greatness, a fount of European culture whose cities belonged to mankind, where one might discern both hope and foreboding for the future, but often found only languor. Petrarch had raised a language and with it a national identity; and elsewhere Byron echoes the song of a modern who yearned for 'the immortality of independence', Vincenzo de Filicaia:

> Italia! oh Italia! thou who hast
> The fatal gift of beauty, which became
> A funeral dower of present woes and past,
> On thy sweet brow is sorrow plough'd by shame.

Nowhere, Byron reminds us, did history so pointedly expose the transience and futility of human endeavour as in this 'mother of dead empires':

> The Niobe of nations! there she stands,
> Childless and crownless, in her voiceless woe;
> An empty urn within her wither'd hands,
> Whose holy dust was scatter'd long ago.

Perhaps Turner was thinking of these lines also when he added a vase to the left foreground of the picture.

For Byron and for Turner, himself a pessimistic student of fallen empires who had already painted the changed fortunes of Greece and Carthage, there were lessons to learn in Italy, not least for their own nation at the height of her powers. Turner of all people would have responded to Byron's apprehensions in Venice, whose lot

> Is shameful to the nations, – most of all,
> Albion! to thee: the Ocean queen should not
> Abandon ocean's children; in the fall
> Of Venice think of thine, despite thy watery wall.

Dedicating the fourth canto of *Childe Harold* to Hobhouse, Byron had spoken of the fate awaiting his own countrymen as a just political retribution for the diplomacy that had left so much of Italy enslaved. Turner would doubtless have drawn the line here, preferring instead the vision of historical inevitability that struck the Childe as he scrambled over the broken ruins of Rome:

> There is the moral of all human tales;
> 'Tis but the same rehearsal of the past,
> First Freedom, and then Glory – when that fails,
> Wealth, vice, corruption, – barbarism at last.
> And History, with all her volumes vast,
> Hath but *one* page.

For all his strictures on Turner's partial understanding of the Byronic mentality, Ruskin did once recognise the relevance of the poet's parable of human life – and, appropriately, when writing of Turner's 'Italy':

> I said that Turner painted the labour of men, their sorrow, and their
> death. This he did nearly in the same tones of mind which prompted
> Byron's Childe Harold, and the loveliest result of his art, in the
> central period of it, was an effort to express on a single canvas the
> meaning of that poem.[15]

Here surely is Ruskin's most pertinent contribution to an understanding of the picture. Far from making only a passing reference to Byron, this noble landscape with its rich symbolism, its melancholy and poignant beauty, is a true illustration of Byron's lines, of the stanzas that follow them, and of the sentiments they comprehend.

Childe Harold was again acknowledged in the complete title of Turner's 'Bright Stone of Honour (Ehrenbreitstein), and Tomb of Marceau', exhibited at the Academy in 1835 (p.93). This was painted for Turner's friend and engraver John Pye, who had already engraved twelve plates after his work, the first being another poetic subject, 'Pope's Villa' (1809–10). Pye presumably hoped to capitalise on the trend for landscape illustrations to Byron that had by now been encouraged by the smaller plates published by Murray and the Findens (nos.46 *et seq.*), and it seems that this project was the first for large-scale engravings of separate plates that Turner considered in the 1830s, although in fact the result was not published until 1845. It is unclear whether Turner or Pye chose the subject, which was apparently first intended to be realised in watercolour rather than oil. Like

'Waterloo', which had been published in mezzotint by F. C. Lewis in 1830, 'Ehrenbreitstein' refers to one of the more specifically contemporary passages in *Childe Harold* III and looked back to Turner's tour of the Low Countries and Rhine in 1817.

Turner's visit had already provided him with material for two fine watercolours of Ehrenbreitstein, one of which, showing the demolition of the great fortress (no.87), had been engraved by Pye in 1828 for the *Literary Souvenir;* the other had been engraved by Robert Wallis to accompany Ralph Bernal's 'Recollections of Ehrenbreitstein, a Tale' in the *Keepsake* for 1833. For Pye's new plate, Turner chose Byron's account of an earlier episode and a fallen hero. General Marceau – like the Maid of Saragossa whom Byron had also celebrated in *Childe Harold* (no.11) – was one of those protagonists in Napoleon's wars whose youth and selfless bravery won them a place in a European pantheon of heroes regardless of which side they had fought on. Both humane and courageous, Marceau had died young, from an Austrian bullet at the Battle of Altenkirchen. In tribute to his past career, the Austrian army had joined with the French in honouring his burial near Coblenz (General Hoche, another distinguished soldier of Napoleon's early campaigns, whose monument at Weissenthurm Turner had also drawn in 1817, was laid alongside). The stone pyramid, as much a 'bright stone of honour' as Ehrenbreitstein itself, is the memorial, and may still be seen today. Describing it, Byron joined with the Austrians in paying tribute to a great opponent:

> Beneath its base are heroes' ashes hid,
> Our enemy's – but let that not forbid
> Honour to Marceau!
> … he was Freedom's champion.

Shown with the passage including these lines, Turner's picture was said by the *Spectator* to be 'a splendid tribute of genius to one of the champions of freedom'. Besides being a shimmering evocation of natural beauty, cast in Turner's most brilliant and gauzy colours, it documented history and respected Byron's moral perspective. Around the monument are the ranks of the two armies whose artillery had fired a volley in Marceau's honour at his burial, and the tents of the general's former headquarters are spread nearby, while in the foreground Austrian soldiers in their white and scarlet uniforms have come to pay their respects. Turner had in fact shortened Byron's lines to omit his explanation that the 'mourners were two hosts, his friends and foes', and his description of the general's death 'falling for France, whose rights he battled to resume', perhaps to dilute any taint of revolutionary sympathy; nevertheless the picture clearly speaks Byron's messages of respect for an honourable foe, and of a wider Europeanism.

Turner's other Byronic paintings were all Italian. For two of the Roman and Venetian subjects, he adapted the lines that immediately followed the passage from *Childe Harold* IV he had quoted with 'Italy';

> The moon is up, and yet it is not night;
> Sunset divides the day with her.

The divided image is quintessentially Byronic, and perfectly fitted to Turner's own purposes. 'Modern Rome – Campo Vaccino' (no.37) was exhibited at the Academy in 1839. It was painted as a companion to 'Ancient Rome: Agrippina Landing with the Ashes of Germanicus' (Tate Gallery; B&J 378) to form a contrasted pair. Turner had already shown 'Ancient' and 'Modern Italy' in 1838, and both pairs, like his earlier pictures of Greece and Carthage, are concerned with antique cultures, or with Empire, in triumph and decay. In neither of these pairs does Turner make his meanings specific, though it is implied that the wheel of history can turn in the arts, religion and political morality as well as in physical decay from classic grandeur to pastoral waste. Thomson, the Augustan idol of both Byron and Turner, had described in his great poem *Liberty* (1735) the establishment and later erosion of the principle in Ancient Rome; its absence in modern Italy, where Austria ruled the north and a corrupt papacy was strangling the Eternal City, was plain to all and had been documented with brutal clarity by Byron. Thomson may have been a source for Turner's poignant comparisons of Italian past and present, but the painter could appeal to a long and rich tradition, and for his second pair he used a verse of his own besides the two lines from Byron. 'Ancient Rome', presenting an episode in the city's early decline, the return of the ashes of Germanicus whose line was to produce Caligula and Nero, was given Turner's own image of dwindling light:

> the yellow Tiber glimmers to her beam,
> Even while the sun is setting.

'Modern Rome', in which the Forum, potent symbol of past greatness and of independent debate, crumbles to ruin and sinks into dusk, received Byron's description of the rising moon, changed, by accident or design, to carry a slightly more positive inflection:

> The sun as yet divides the day with her.

For both Turner and Byron, there was great beauty as well as sadness in Modern Rome. What may come with the approaching night is left to our imagination but Turner's subtle change from 'sunset' to 'sun' may serve to remind us that all is not yet lost – neither of light nor of hope.

Just how deliberate were Turner's misquotations or adaptations is a question that arises again when, in 1844, he exhibited 'Approach to Venice' (no.39) with the same passage, retaining 'sun' but further changing the verb to the more loaded 'disputes'. This may seem a minor alteration, the result of forgetfulness, but it is worth considering as characteristic of an attitude to Venice that was in fact totally Byronic. Turner may have felt the more free to adapt the lines in that Byron had not written them to apply to Venice at all, but to embrace a wider panorama of Italy. Moreover 'Approach to Venice' seems the least specifically Byronic of Turner's Byron paintings, and indeed the quotation was secondary to a longer and more appropriate one from Rogers's *Italy*, describing a languid arrival in the city by gondola. Other stanzas from *Childe Harold*, we may feel, would have served better to accompany this ethereal gathering of craft in the darkling lagoon. Yet still we should puzzle over that word 'disputes'. The truth, surely, is that Turner saw Venice exactly as Byron did – as a city further fallen from past greatness, more truly enslaved, than any in Italy, but also more transcendant in its beauty and possessed of a greater ability to bounce back and keep her spirit alive in the theatre or the opera, in Carnival and fireworks.

In 1840, to accompany his 'Venice, Bridge of Sighs' (no.38), Turner had chosen (and slightly abbreviated) the powerful lines with which Byron had begun *Childe Harold* IV:

> I stood in Venice, on the Bridge of Sighs;
> A palace and a prison on each hand.

The opposing images, while drawn exactly from the topography of Venice, immediately take us to the heart of Byron's pattern of thought. Indeed it was in his stanzas on Venice that he laid out the central messages of the poem. The palace and the prison are perfectly balanced, symbolising the grim realities underlying a sumptuous past. Venice itself, under Austrian rule, had become a prison for its citizens. No city had toppled further from its former glory, and Byron systematically contrasts past and present and evokes the loveliness still clinging to the crumbling fabric. He views her from afar, 'a sea Cybele, fresh from ocean', and from painfully close; he reconstructs her fabled history in indulgent language, and describes her present woes, concluding

> Those days are gone – but Beauty still is here.
> States fall, arts fade – but Nature doth not die.

Byron, who made Venice his home for several years, could not see the city in black and white. It was for him a compound of echoes and associations, of triumph and sadness, beauty and dereliction, of which a picture had first been formed through reading – 'Otway, Radcliffe, Schiller, Shakespeare's art' – then modified by observation and broadened by imaginative reconstruction – 'I can repeople with the past'. His Venice becomes a universe, and his rousing assertion in the Venetian canto of the eternal power of nature – a concept Turner would at once embrace – was followed by a further reminder, which must have sprung from his own essentially joyous experiences in Venice but also carried a universal weight

> Nor yet forget how Venice once was dear,
> The pleasant place of all festivity,
> The revel of the earth, the masque of Italy!

These were the lines Turner condensed for a quotation to attach to George Hollis's large engraving, made in 1842 after his painting of 'Juliet and her Nurse' of 1836, and retitled simply 'St Mark's Place, Venice (Moonlight)' (no.40). The passage was perfect for the picture. In this, Turner's final published acknowledgment of Byron, all sadness and foreboding are banished; beneath *this* moon is a city of dazzling light and myriad entertainments. In the city where Turner had followed closest and most often in Byron's footsteps, he had found at last the essence of Byron's feeling for the place – what Michael Foot, most sensitive of modern Byronists, has justly called 'a joyousness, an exuberance, which was much more truly Byronic than any affected melancholy'.[16]

BYRON ENGRAVED

Apart from his paintings, Turner's main contribution to the iconography of Byron consisted in the series of landscape and vignette designs he made for the Finden brothers and for John Murray. These appeared in two publications, Finden's *Landscape Illustrations* to Byron, and Murray's edition of Moore's *Life and Works* of the poet, both of which commenced publication in 1832, the year 'Childe Harold's Pilgrimage – Italy' (no.36) was shown at the Royal Academy. The history of these two projects has been much confused. The sheer number of editions of Byron produced in the decades after the poet's death seems to have deterred Rawlinson, when compiling his magnum opus on Turner's prints, from a proper investigation of the Byron subjects, and later writers have added errors to his ambiguities. In particular, the myth has arisen that seven of Turner's landscape subjects – most of them Greek – date from 'the earliest time when he worked as a book-illustrator, about 1823–4', and were engraved for an edition of Byron published by Murray in 1825; scholars differ as to the substance of this edition, some stating it comprised eleven volumes, others seven. In fact it can safely be said that no such edition existed. The following account may, it is hoped, go some way to setting the record straight.

Far from pre-dating Turner's most active phase as a book-illustrator, his Byron designs belong precisely to it. None seems to have been started before 1830, and all were apparently finished by 1833. There is nothing in the history of the Byron subjects to challenge the view that he graduated to commercial literary illustration from his work from *c.*1826 as a designer for popular annuals like the *Keepsake*. With his other sets of illustrations to Scott, Moore and Campbell, those to Byron sprang largely from the same motive – the publishers' eagerness to capitalise on the phenomenal success achieved for Rogers's hitherto somewhat *recherché* poem *Italy*, by the designs Turner contributed for a 'de luxe' edition published in 1830. Robert Cadell spoke for all his colleagues when in 1831 he assured a sceptical Scott that 'Mr Turner's pencil, will ensure the sale of 8000 of the Poetry – without, not 3000'.

Such inducement was hardly necessary for Byron, whose work remained in heavy demand; if the poet's moral and critical standing had declined after his death, this had not diminished his hold on the popular imagination. Nor was there any lack of illustrated editions. Byron himself had admired the illustrations to *Don Juan* by Richard Westall published in 1820, even declaring 'the brush has beat the poetry', and there were other romantic or sentimental interpretations to choose from. Murray had published designs by Thomas Stothard in an edition of Byron in 1815, (Maria Bicknell sent her future husband Constable a newspaper cutting about them); in 1821 Colnaghi brought out a set of etchings of Byronic subjects by Sir John James Stuart; and four years later there appeared, in parts between June and July, George Clinton's *Memoirs of the Life and Writings of Lord Byron*, with rather perfunctory engravings by George Cruikshank (bound copies were published by James Robins in 1826, no.18). Murray's editions of the poems of 1830 and 1831 included sentimental subjects after Henry Corbould, whose interpretation of Byron had first appeared in the Academy in 1814, and Henry Richter.

This list does not pretend to be complete, but will at least indicate the predominant character of Byron illustration – a character that also extended to the majority of exhibited Byron subjects in oil and watercolour. Most artists chose dramatic or sentimental figure subjects, favouring the Oriental tales for their picturesque possibilities or singling out exotic females who could be rendered in varying states of emotional excess or with thinly veiled eroticism. These 'Byron beauties' were perhaps the most contemporary in feeling, in that they appealed to the readership of the popular annuals, but the interpretation of the narrative scenes was often old-fashioned, rooted in the tradition of such late eighteenth century publications as Macklin's *Poet's Gallery*, Bell's *British Poets* or Sharpe's *Classics*. The illustrators made little attempt to assimilate the moods or settings of Byron's poetry; its sense of place, its treatment of nature or landscape, seemed to elude them even though the Academy had seen realisations of Byronic landscape since 1817, and John Varley had won the premium at the Water-Colour Society in 1821 with an epic watercolour of the 'place of a thousand tombs' from *The Bride of Abydos*.

Long before he was called upon to illustrate Byron commercially, Turner had struck a different and more profound note in the single illustration to *The Giaour* that he made for Walter Fawkes (p.97). This was one of a small group of illustrations to modern poetry, presumably to support a compilation of family favourites by Byron, Scott and Moore, the 'three poets in three kingdoms born' of whom Turner also provided a vignette frontispiece. Four subjects were selected from Scott, from *Marmion, Rokeby, The Lady of the Lake* and *The Lay of the Last Minstrel*; all were topographical or architectural, with the relevant quotations incorporated into the designs. From Moore there was one subject, from *Lalla Rookh*, and from Byron one built around a shortened version of the line concluding the opening passage of *The Giaour*, ''T'is living Greece no more'. In this famous passage, Byron had used a newly dead corpse, lifelike but lifeless, as a metaphor for the state of Greece as it languished under Turkish domination. In verses of almost unbearable poignancy, impelled by the dialectic thrust of opposing images and a metre as solemn and measured as a funeral bell –

> He who hath bent him o'er the dead
> Ere the first day of death is fled;
> The first dark day of nothingness,
> The last of danger and distress

– he built up to the point that Turner chose:

> Such is the aspect of this shore;
> 'T'is Greece – but living Greece no more!

Of the poetic subjects for Fawkes known today, that from *The Giaour* is the only one to bear a date, 1822; it is therefore Turner's earliest known watercolour illustrating Byron. It affords a remarkable premonition of Turner's associationist approach to literary illustration, containing elements that are not precisely to be found in the text but help to expand its ideas. Turner's approach to Byron – as indeed to literary subjects generally – can already be seen to have been enriched by his wider reading, both inside and beyond the work in question; by his own historical interests; by the recollections of friends; and also, one assumes in this case, by the concerns of his patron, whose European outlook and libertarian principles presumably extended to philhellenism – this was exactly the period when Byron's friend Hobhouse was drumming up support for the London Greek Committee.

Within the convenient format of an upright landscape, Turner has combined a view of the Acropolis, symbol of a once-glorious city state, with a foreground tragically contrasting a fragment of the Parthenon frieze with a tableau of modern servitude – two shackled Greek slaves watched by a gloating Turk. The nearest source for Turner's motif may be the footnote added by Byron to a later passage of the poem, explaining that Athens was then the property of 'the slave of the seraglio and the guardian of the women'. As we have seen in his paintings, Turner's Byronic renderings were rarely restricted to the actual text quoted, but depended on a wider appreciation; yet how marvellously his imagery amplifies the meanings behind the line. Bondage, servitude, the collapse of a sublime cultural and political civilisation within the ruins of its former greatness – all these Byronic fundamentals are here, and Turner has not failed to imply an ambiguity as to whether the beautiful slave in the foreground is languishing or indeed dead; she casts a reddish shadow, and the scimitar of her Turkish guard is slung menacingly nearby. Turner had surely not missed Byron's other note, expanding his image of 'the look by death reveal'd': 'in death from a stab the countenance preserves its traits of feeling or ferocity, and the mind its bias, to the last'.

Turner's exposition of *The Giaour*, then, is such as to justify the highest expectations of his later Byron illustrations. Like his first Byron subject, 'The Field of Waterloo' (no.35), it is an uncompromisingly modern image, and one that looked out to the condition of a wider European world. It displays all his gifts of investing a view with a wealth of meaning and reference, even though he had never seen Athens and had no personal experience of its current miseries. The same gifts would be required in large measure when he was commissioned to illustrate Byron for publication. As in his watercolour for Fawkes, his task would be the realisation of the Byronic landscape – the Europe through which the poet and his heroes travelled. Some of it he had seen himself, so that he could fully empathise with Byron's feelings and musings. Other places, like Athens, he would reconstruct from the sketches of travellers, just as he had by then created a convincing Italy for James Hakewill's *Picturesque Tour of Italy* from the author's own drawings (Byron owned a copy), and had painted the temple at Aegina after Gally Knight. It was a task for which he was uniquely qualified, and which served an obvious need.

Finden's *Landscape Illustrations*

It was probably William Finden who first recognised the potential for illustrating Byron with places rather than narrative episodes. For the general reader, Byron was as much as anything a poet of travel, and one whose own peregrinations, coloured with the romance of scandal, exile and his death in the campaign for Greek independence, were as fascinating as his heroes'. The readers of the popular annuals were already greedy consumers of travellers' tales and accompanying views engraved after well-known artists, and a spread from the *Landscape Annual* for 1831, showing a view of Byron's Venetian home, the Palazzo Mocenigo, facing some anecdotal (if gratuitously moralistic) text by Thomas Roscoe, indicates how readily the poet might be assimilated into the convention (no.8). It was a logical step to illustrate the poetry itself with a series of views and further biographical notes on the author. Such was Finden's first idea. No doubt it seemed foolproof, if necessarily expensive; and perhaps the only surprise is that it had not been attempted earlier. Finden was able to develop this project at the same time as he was working for Murray on a related scheme, the illustration of Moore's *Life and Works* of Byron for a popular edition in monthly parts, and it was perhaps through his influence that this latter also concentrated on landscape subjects. For both projects, Finden and Murray recruited Turner.

Turner had already worked with both Finden and Murray. Finden's younger brother Edward had engraved Turner's 'Bolton Abbey' for the *Literary Souvenir* in 1826; Murray had shared in the publication of Turner's *Picturesque Views of the Southern Coast of England* from 1814, and brought out Hakewill's *Italy* with his illustrations – one, as we have seen, placed near an apt quotation from *Childe Harold* – from 1818. The Findens and Murray, however, were quite new to each other. William engraved Sanders's portrait of Byron as the frontispiece to Murray's first edition of Moore's life of the poet, published in 1830 (no.41), and it was while carrying out this project – a highly sensitive one as the portrait belonged to Hobhouse, who was characteristically fussed about the outcome – that Finden conceived his own Byron project. He had himself contributed the engravings after Stothard to accompany Turner's vignette views in the memorable edition of Rogers's *Italy*, so was in a position to appreciate the advantage of securing Turner's collaboration. His dealings over the engraving after Sanders gave him an opportunity to press for a further advantage, the involvement of Hobhouse himself. With such a powerful combination, he persuaded Murray to share in the plan. But soon his problems began.

Hobhouse was at first encouraging – so much so as to give Finden the impression, quite wrongly as it turned out, that he would provide some notes of his own from recollections of Byron and of the places they had visited together. Hobhouse even drafted a list of subjects, and Finden lost no time in applying to Turner and other artists to draw them. Matters were in train by 2 October 1830, when Finden wrote to Hobhouse asking not only for his comments on the engraving after Sanders for Moore, but also for news of his progress on the text; he was 'extremely anxious to shew you the progress we have made with the Illustrations … May I ask if you have commenced with your intended account? Since the publication of Mr. Galt, it has become more than ever desirable'.[17] The reference to John Galt might have been calculated to stir Hobhouse to action, if only to set the record straight, for Hobhouse had been in angry correspondence with Galt over the many inaccuracies in his newly published biography of Byron. In fact, however, while approving Finden's engraving after Sanders, Hobhouse now withdrew from any commitment the engraver thought he had made. On 6 October Finden wrote back that 'you have relieved me from one source of uneasiness, but … created another and a greater'. Hobhouse had claimed that the proposed illustrations would be self-sufficient, and that the role of any author would appear secondary. Finden disagreed:

> Without your important part (to which the Illustrations would be but as auxilliaries) I should be bereft of my sheet anchor, and should tremble to launch them. In every way I view the great importance of the literary part of the work, not only to myself personally, but to the public, for coming from you, it would not only at once raise the character of my Illustrations but would put every other work relative to Ld Byrons Memoirs out of demand, and become a work of reference.

By this time Finden had commissioned at least two drawings from Turner:

> I think I shall be able to complete the Engravings for the first portion in Jany or early Feby next and should of course be anxious to publish as soon after as possible. Mr Turner has undertaken to make the Drawings of Malta and Gibraltar <u>from very fine sketches</u> and I expect them immediately upon his return to Town.

This is the most concrete evidence we have for dating the landscape series. Murray's involvement in the scheme had apparently begun in August 1830, for his ledgers, preserved at Albemarle Street, describe transactions for it between that month and October 1831 – although without specific dates for each. The purchase of the Malta and Gibraltar subjects are recorded at £24 3s. each; two other Turner subjects are listed, of Athens and the Temple of Minerva, at £21 each. The ledgers further record the sale of all these at a fairly significant loss, Malta and Gibraltar only making £18 2s. 3d. each. Interestingly, the project is described as being for illustrations to *Childe Harold* only; the heading reads 'Landscape Illustrations to Byron … Ch. Harold', and the accounts are in the name of the 'Proprietors of Childe Harold Work'.

Finden's correspondence, however, suggests that he saw the scheme in a somewhat different light – one that would explain why not all Turner's drawings specifically illustrate *Childe Harold* or any other poem, and why Hobhouse's withdrawal left him in such a 'dilemma'. By 25 February, when he wrote to plead with Hobhouse, he had discussed the problem with Murray, who shared his concern. There were now, he told Hobhouse, many of the subjects 'already engraved, taken from the list you suggested' and many of them

> would be utterly useless, unless accompanied by the descriptive narrative you gave me to expect. I trust you will forgive me (but as this is my first speculation and having already expended £1000 I am

naturally anxious for the results) if I again recall to your memory the
Title you suggested, viz: 'Some account of the Life and Travels of Ld
Byron, from documents hitherto unknown'.

Even short notes would suffice, and Finden now offered a further inducement; he had

> studied how I could (without giving offence by considering you as an
> author in the common understanding of the term) shew you the high
> estimation I entertain of it, and I hope you will not be offended if
> I name the manner in which I always intended to express my
> gratitude. It is that of presenting you with the series of Drawings.
> They may perhaps possess much interest with you, independently of
> their being beautiful works of art, and I trust you will accept them as
> tokens of the feelings I have so imperfectly expressed.

But Finden had underestimated the implacable resistance Hobhouse
showed to all who would publish on his old friend. Unmoved, Hobhouse
replied on 30 January:

> I will not do it. That's final. I have told you so fifty times before and
> if you press me any more I shall get angry – your list is a very good
> one, and the subjects may all be described by any decent performer
> by extracting from Byron's poems, Moore's life, Galt – & my Travels
> – so do not be afraid for your speculation, but go to work in a
> business-like way, with Mr. Murray, or, if he refuses to deal, with
> Mr Colburn, or Mr. Longman or Mr. Anybody Else – Pray be kind
> enough to consider this a final answer, for I really cannot write or say
> any more on the subject.

Far from refusing to deal, Murray was already involved, but finding himself in a very embarassing position. He had taken a share in Finden's
speculation, but wished neither to proceed without Hobhouse's text nor to
upset Byron's old friend. Naturally there could be no question of Hobhouse receiving the drawings, and the ledgers show that they had been
sold by the time the correspondence was resumed in November, with a
final plea from Murray to Hobhouse:

> feeling as I do the surety that you would not willingly – or knowingly,
> do an unkind thing to me – after so long an acquaintance … I there-
> fore venture to state the serious inconvenience which I am suffering
> under, in consequence of the apparent disinclination to fulfil your
> 'Royal Word' by communicating the promised literary communication,
> to the series of beautiful engravings which have been prepared by
> your suggestion to illustrate it – It was entirely owing to the assurance
> of Messr⁵ Finden of your voluntary offer to contribute an original
> account of Lord Byron and of his travels, that I was induced to take a

half share in this expensive project – The Drawings were almost all made after your own desire, and of which I have an elaborate list in your own handwriting – The Engravings from these by the first Artist are perfectly beautiful, and would, I assure you, do justice to the Narrative … it would become one of the most popular works in the higher circles of literature, that has been published for many years.

Hobhouse's reply does not appear to have survived, but it clearly blamed Finden for holding him to a promise he had never made. On 8 November Finden wrote to Hobhouse in unconcealed rage:

Mr Murray has just handed over to me a letter which he has received from you, wherein you charge me of disingenuous conduct and misrepresentation … I feel myself called upon once more … to recall to your mind the History of the transaction. When I first waited upon you … I casually mentioned to you that I was about illustrating the Poems of Ld Byron topographically … You inquired who was to make the descriptions and … immediately said that it was a thing you should like to do above all other … that you would consider about it. I of course joyfully embraced the project.

Finden then acknowledged that Hobhouse had changed his mind after deciding that text would seem secondary to plates, but further recalled that the revised title suggested by Hobhouse, 'from documents hitherto unpublished', and the obscure nature of some of the subjects he proposed for the illustrations, implied his continuing interest:

Now as no other than yourself was in possession of such documents, what other conclusion could be drawn, than, that it was your intention to write the account? Particularly when, as I had some difficulty in procuring sketches of some of the subjects contained in the list you gave me (and which did not illustrate the poems) you said, that they were indispensably necessary, as you had some interesting anecdotes to relate respecting them. These have become a dead loss.

As for Hobhouse's charge of 'outrageous conduct' in his letter to Murray,

I can't accuse myself of any act that could give a shadow of justice to your accusation … Mr M. has been cognisent of all that has transpired … neither the slightest colouring nor misrepresentation has been used by me. I feel myself incapable of such conduct and fling back the accusation with disdain.

If we allow for naivety and inexperience on Finden's part – this was indeed his first 'speculation' – and for Hobhouse's habitual obstinacy over Byronic publications, it is difficult to know who was most responsible for this impasse. The drawings were now made, not only by Turner but by other artists besides, and the engravings completed. Finden's expenditure had been considerable – indeed as he reminded Hobhouse, he had at first carried all the expenses before Murray's intervention, and in Turner's case, the Albemarle Street ledgers show that Murray only paid for four of the drawings. Neither Finden nor Murray could recoup their outlay without publication, but on what terms? Murray's quandary must have been the greater in that he was now well advanced with his separate project (also involving both Finden and Turner) for illustrating Moore's *Life and Works*. It was important that the series initiated by Finden himself should not steal its thunder. Finden meanwhile, presumably fearful that Murray would withdraw his support altogether, seems to have opened separate negotiations with Charles Tilt, the publisher whom Turner was to take to court in 1833 over his unauthorised use of his illustrations to Scott.

Murray may have been less than pleased to receive Tilt's letter of 5 October, announcing his intention to commence publication of the *Illustrations* in January; 'I thought it right as an act of courtesy to inform you … though I do not anticipate any objection … such a work will attach some additional importance and publicity if that were needed, to the new edition you have announced'. Finden upset Murray further by proposing to add plates, including the seventeen vignettes after Turner engraved by his brother Edward, intended for the *Life and Works*. On 19 November Murray wrote to Finden, more in sorrow than in anger:

> I have consulted all the most honourable men in the trade respecting your intention of publishing against my will a series of illustrations to my Edition of Lord Byron's Works – and there is but one opinion as to the impropriety of your persisting in this intention and of the absolute impossibility of my sanctioning it – Discussion upon the subject is therefore useless – but I trust that your sense of justice will enable me to continue – what I always wish to be, your friend.

When the *Illustrations* finally appeared, they did so with both Murray and Tilt named on the wrappers, which could hardly have been done without sanction from Albemarle Street. Perhaps a letter from Hobhouse, of 21 November, was the last straw that persuaded Murray that Finden had indeed been hard done by and deserved a compromise. With singular tactlessness, Hobhouse wrote to propose almost exactly the sort of text he had refused to supply for Finden; he had for some time been 'reconstructing' his notes on *Childe Harold*, together with material gathered afterwards in Italy, and offered two or three volumes, thinking he might 'produce something not altogether without use or attraction'. Indeed; but Murray could hardly have missed the irony.

The *Illustrations* were first published in fourteen monthly parts, in paper wrappers, from 16 January 1832. Each part contained five plates, one or two being portraits, and it was explained that advice would be given on the proper arrangement on completion of the series. The cost was proudly set at 'no more than Two Shillings and Sixpence' for a quarto edition; one in Royal quarto with plates on india paper was also issued at 7s. 6d. per part. The announcement in the first part chose its words carefully: following the 'general admiration' for advance specimens of the plates engraved for the edition of Moore, 'Mr. MURRAY has been induced to announce a series of ILLUSTRATIONS ... executed by those eminent artists, William and Edward Finden, on a scale of beauty and cheapness never before attempted in this country'. Acknowledging the forthcoming *Life and Works*, the puff continued that in issuing the two series 'concurrently', Murray hoped not only to display 'the actual state of Painting and the Fine Arts in England', but also to show that 'upon the scale of cheapness, we are able to compete with our continental neighbours'. Such an affordable illustrated edition would surely, when assembled complete, eradicate the need for 'the garbled and imperfect portions of BYRON's writings, which are incessantly issuing from the presses of Paris, Brussels and Hamburgh'.

Nine landscape subjects after Turner were published, all but three in Edward Finden's engravings. The views of Gibraltar (no.46), Malta (no.50), Athens (no.47), and the Temple of Minerva (today accredited to Poseidon) at Cape Colonna (Sunium) (no.51), are all named in Hobhouse's list and itemised in the Murray accounts; the others, of the tomb of Cecilia Metella (no.56), Rhodes (no.55), the Drachenfels (no.53), Cephalonia (no.57) and Negropont (no.58), are not named in either place but are clearly uniform; presumably they were Finden's share of the project, and listed separately. The majority are, as originally intended, illustrations to *Childe Harold*, three being for the second canto and two for the fourth, but others, of Malta, Rhodes, Cephalonia and Negropont, must have been selected with Hobhouse's biographical contributions in mind since they do not directly support the poem and sometimes relate very tenuously even to Byron's life – Negropont, for example, was a place Hobhouse regretted his friend had *failed* to visit! It was these which, in Finden's telling phrase, had lost their 'sheet anchor' by Hobhouse's withdrawal, and the situation was the more galling in that Finden had gone to considerable trouble to provide Turner with working sketches by experienced travellers.

The preponderance of Greek subjects meant that Turner could not work from personal experience, and was bound to rely on secondary material, be it drawings, personal recollections or his own reading. He already knew Gally Knight, whose boyhood connection with Byron had been renewed in Greece, and Charles Eastlake, whose travels there in 1818 had taken him to many Byronic places – Aegina, Sunium, Corinth, Delphi, Castri – and brought him into contact with some of the poet's old acquaintances including Lusieri. In Scotland in 1818, Turner had met another distinguished artist and philhellene, Hugh 'Grecian' Williams, and, in connection with a project for illustrating a publication on the temple at Aegina, was now on close professional terms with the leader of the Anglo-German team that had excavated there, the architect C.R. Cockerell. It was perhaps on Cockerell's advice that Turner acquired a work that must have greatly helped him with his Byronic illustrations, the Revd T.S. Hughes's *Travels in Sicily, Greece and Albania* (1820), wherein indeed there was occasional mention of Byron (no.29); and Williams's *Select Views in Greece with Classical Illustrations*, published in 1829, might also have been added to his library with the Byron project in mind. Among the sketches supplied to Turner specifically for it, some could provide yet more links with Byron and his circle. Views of the Acropolis, Sunium and Negropont were provided by Thomas Allason, an artist and architect who had travelled in Greece and known Gally Knight and Cockerell in Athens, while that of Gibraltar was supplied by George Reinagle, a marine painter who in 1827 had accompanied Sir Edward Codrington's fleet in the eastern Mediterranean during the campaign for Greek independence.

With such a wealth of personal and documentary sources, it is hardly surprising that Turner did not feel constrained by working at second hand. In fact he responded with some splendid realisations, especially of Athens with cavalry in the foreground (no.47), and of Sunium (no.51) whose mingled associations from Plato to the poet Falconer, pointed out in *Childe Harold*, and whose citation in the song to Greek liberty in *Don Juan* – supplemented no doubt by Eastlake's recollections of a two-day stay in 1818 – also moved Turner to a magnificent large watercolour (no.28). It must however be admitted that the subjects where Turner was on surer personal ground, the views of Rome and the Rhine (nos.56, 53), are of exceptional quality; for the first he could recall his observations in Italy in 1819 and an earlier rendering of the same subject for Hakewill (no.34), and for the second, his Rhine tour of 1817 and a watercolour of the same place made for Fawkes that year (no.86).

fig.7 'Rome, the Tomb of Cecilia Metella', *c.*1832, watercolour (w 1214). *Manchester City Art Galleries*

With the nine landscape subjects, Finden, Tilt and Murray also issued plates by Turner and others recycled from Murray's edition of Moore's *Life and Works*. The Byronic relevance of these was clear enough, but it was apparent that the landscapes that did not truly illustrate *Childe Harold* needed explanation. In the end William Brockedon, whose *Illustrations to the Passes of the Alps* had been handsomely engraved by Edward Finden and published by Murray (1827–9), was commissioned to provide supplementary text (no.56). Alas he proved unequal to the challenge, for his captions are both brief and bland. Although he was on safe ground with the plate of 'Cephalonia', the island where Byron 'began his operations in the Greek war of independence', he could only remark of 'Negropont' that it gave a sense of the coastal scenery of Euboea, while 'Rhodes' he failed to explain at all. His annotations appeared in a reprint of the *Illustrations*, published by Murray in 1833. For this edition, the irrepressible Finden announced 'a new and beautiful Frontispiece by Turner', but this was the Gibralter subject he already had in hand (no.46).

Moore's *Life and Works*

Thomas Moore's *Letters and Journals of Lord Byron with Notices of his Life* first came out in 1830. Moore had trodden a delicate path between saying too much and too little, and had done his best to respect the memory of his friend and fellow poet. He had met with the usual obstructions from Hobhouse, but had struggled manfully on to produce what was, by the biographical standards of the time, a most creditable work. Murray paid Moore lavishly for the text, and the book was expensive. There were no illustrations in the first edition save for Finden's engraving of the Sanders portrait. By the end of 1831 Murray decided to target a much wider market, and to issue Moore's text with Byron's works in monthly parts at a modest price, illustrated with frontispieces and title-page plates. The Findens were commissioned to obtain and engrave the illustrations, and a number of artists were engaged including, besides Turner, Richard Westall, George Cattermole, Clarkson Stanfield and J. D. Harding. They were to produce vignettes, chiefly of landscape and topographical subjects, thus following the practice initiated by Finden on a reduced format. Murray assumed that the expenses incurred in commissioning this material would be amply repaid by massive sales, and he was right. When the series was almost complete, in February 1833, he wrote to the son of George Crabbe, whose work he was planning to issue in similar form, that 'a great taste for favourite authors has been created by bringing them out splendidly embellished exceedingly cheap, and in monthly parts'.

On 13 February 1832 Murray contracted an agreement with Turner stating that he would pay him fifty guineas if he used his Byron drawings 'for the Illustration of any other works' (no.44). The previous month the first volume of the series had been published. Volumes then appeared monthly until April 1833, and the last was issued in June, making a total of seventeen. Murray's accounts show that the first payment for any of the drawings was made in December 1831, to Westall, and to Turner for his 'Plain of Troy' (£26 5s., plus two guineas for a working sketch by William Page). 'Troy' (no.63) did not appear until July 1832, in the seventh volume. The first Turner subject to appear in the series was 'Santa Maria della Spina, Pisa' (no.60 and fig.8), in May 1832 in the fifth volume. Murray paid £28 7s. for the drawing, and ten guineas for 'selecting and procuring' it. Presumably the latter fee went to the Findens; all Turner's designs for the series were engraved by Edward. The last of Turner's drawings listed in Murray's accounts were 'The School of Homer, Scio' (no.82 and fig.9) and 'The Castellated Rhine' (no.83), which appeared in June 1833 in

fig.8 'Santa Maria della Spina, Pisa', *c.*1832, watercolour (w 1219). *Visitors of the Ashmolean Museum, Oxford*

the seventeenth volume. Throughout the project, prices paid for the draw-ings had ranged up to a maximum of £31 10s., and engraving costs (apparently for two plates each) had varied between £27 and £37 5s. 6d.; the ten guineas for 'selecting and procuring' had been standard.

The subjects, all treated in vignette, covered a good deal of familiar ground for Turner – the Netherlands, the Alps, the Rhineland and Italy; for the Italian scenes, he was able to repeat a formula he had already used very successfully for Rogers. For unfamiliar subjects in Greece and Turkey he was again provided with working drawings, by William Page and by the promising young architect Charles Barry, who had travelled in the East between 1817 and 1820, part of the time with Eastlake whose own recol-lections of Byronic places like the Castalian Spring at Delphi – where he had found Byron's name in a little chapel – Turner must again have con-sulted. Not surprisingly, the places Turner knew best were rendered most convincingly and displayed his gifts for concision and allusion within a small compass at their best.

It must be remembered that Turner's designs were intended to decorate the beginnings of the volumes, to create a mood and stimulate the imagi-nation of the reader, rather than to relate closely to the text. Turner was clearly under the impression that he was evoking Byron's life as much as his works – on 2 September 1831 he had written to Edward Finden from Oban, offering to collect Scottish scenes from the poet's childhood such as the 'Lin of Don' (*sic*) – but although the results call both equally to mind, they rarely illustrate specific episodes in Moore's biography or in the poems. Even when they do, they do so in a general way, and can some-times be interchangeable with other passages or even other illustrations. For example, 'The Gate of Theseus' (no.62) and 'Plain of Troy' (no.63) are difficult to pin down. Within the seventh volume, where both appeared, the former must relate if at all to *The Maid of Athens*, while the latter, with its stormy sky, can only be associated with *Stanzas Composed during a Thunderstorm* (actually set near Zitza); on the other hand the Gate stood near Byron's Athenian lodgings, so might have been better placed near Moore's life, and the Plain is mentioned several times in other volumes, in biographical particulars or in *Don Juan*. 'Waterloo from Hougoumont' (no.75), Turner's latest and certainly powerful rendering of the dead after the battle, is to be connected with a line from *The Age of Bronze*, published with it in the fourteenth volume, but could equally apply to the Waterloo stanzas in *Childe Harold* or be exchanged with similar subjects prepared for other publications – Scott's *Prose Works* or the *Life of Napoleon*; well might Turner write, when working on his Scott subjects, 'Waterloo I have', and he was surely no more averse to recycling material from one project to another than was his publisher. His two Roman subjects for Byron, 'The Castle of St Angelo' (no.65) and 'Walls of Rome with the Tomb of Caius Sestus' (no.71), might almost have been left over from Rogers's *Italy*, so similar are they in style and approach to his drawings for that book; a similar view of the castle and bridge had been included there, and the tomb – not specifically mentioned by Byron – had been the subject of a descriptive chapter by Rogers.

Turner's designs are somewhat arbitrarily disposed throughout Murray's seventeen volumes, and as a result such connections as he might have hoped to establish are blurred. In some cases it requires a close perusal of the text, the poetry or the accompanying notes to find his likely starting points, and even then we cannot be sure that his brief was not much looser. To some extent the arrangement may have depended on the order in which Turner delivered the drawings; the confinement of the illustrations to frontispiece and title pages imposed its own constraints; and so too did the varied nature of the contents. The length of *Don Juan* – requiring most of the three last volumes – posed special problems, but Murray or Finden deployed Turner's designs in a more random manner than was strictly necessary. In the fifteenth volume appeared a view of Scio (no.77) that relates – albeit tenuously – to mentions of 'Scio's muse' (Homer) and 'Scio's vine' in the 'glorious Ode on the aspirations of Greece after liberty' in the third canto (lxxxvi.2, 9), together with a view of Genoa (no.78) that does not seem to relate to anything in the poem unless it be the journey 'for the port Leghorn' in the second canto (xxiv). 'Cologne' (no.79) and 'St Sophia' (no.80) in the sixteenth volume relate to passages in the tenth canto (lxii) and the fifth (iii) printed therein. The seventeenth volume, on the other hand, contains 'The School of Homer, Scio' (no.82), that might more fittingly refer to the passage in the third canto already mentioned in the fifteenth volume, or to the sixth volume where Moore had described Byron's first visit to the 'School of Homer' in 1823. The other subject in the final volume, 'The Castellated Rhine' (no.83), refers back to the tenth canto (lxii) in the fifteenth volume. Other subjects seem correctly placed. The fifth volume contained the Pisa view (no.60), relating to Moore's account of Byron's residence in the city in 1821–2. In the eighth volume 'Bacharach' (no.64) and the 'Castle of St Angelo' (no.65) are accompaniments to *Childe Harold*, although only the latter subject is specifically named in the poem. The tenth volume contains 'Corinth from the Acropolis' (no.67), setting the stage for *The Siege of Corinth*. The scenes for *Manfred* and *Beppo* are set in the eleventh volume with 'The Bernese Alps' (no.70) and 'The Bridge of Sighs' (no.69), and 'The Walls of Rome' (no.71) in the thirteenth volume realises one of Byron's stage directions for *The Deformed Transformed*. 'Parnassus and Castalian Spring' (no.73) published with 'Waterloo' in the fourteenth volume, relates to *The Island*. The lines of Byron that justified this subject may stand for the rather free approach Turner and his publishers took with the illustrations, allowing them to refer backwards and forwards in the volumes and to create a collective impression of the Byronic world:

Long have I roamed through lands which are not mine,
Adored the Alp, and loved the Apennine,
Revered Parnassus ...
Mix'd Celtic memories with the Phrygian mount,
And Highland linns with Castalie's clear fount.
Forgive me, Homer's universal shade!
Forgive me, Phoebus! that my fancy stray'd.

Ruskin, who greatly loved Turner's illustrations to Rogers for their simplicity and appropriateness, considered those to Byron 'much more laboured, and ... more or less artificial and unequal'.[18] Although Ruskin apparently made no distinction between the landscapes made for Finden and the vignettes for Murray, it is difficult to disagree with his conclusion. The high finish of the vignette drawings is indeed exceptional, while the stock of personal memories that had helped to unite the Rogers series – in Ruskin's words 'simply his own reminiscences ... rapidly and concisely given in right sympathy with the meditative poem they illustrate' – were not always available for many of the Byron subjects. When applying the same method to Byron, that added empathy that sprang from shared experience was often lacking. It is curious nevertheless that Turner did not again assemble the kind of symbolic imagery or narrative, taken from a close reading of the text, that he had offered in his earlier subject from *The Giaour* (p.97). The use of motifs to create a play of reference and allusion usually lies at the heart of Turner's book illustration, and indeed was one area where his mind worked remarkably like Byron's – through just such multiplicity of reference Byron constructed the historical and moral landscape of *Childe Harold*. All the more surprising, perhaps, that Turner did not apply the method very rigorously to his Byron designs. The truth, surely, was that he was working to a short deadline, heavily dependent on second-hand material, and that he was given a list of places rather than particular texts to realise. The craftsmanship and minuteness of touch that he brought to his drawings show that he did not skimp on the project, but to look for a consistent density and richness of interpretation is to expect too much.

Yet in 'The Plain of Troy' (no.63) Ruskin did detect a striking example of Turner's use of typological symbolism, and one that referred as much to the tradition in which Byron wrote as to Byron himself: 'I need not hope', he wrote, 'to make the public believe that the meaning of the sunset contending with the storm is the contest of the powers of Apollo and Athene; but there is nevertheless no question as to the fact. For Turner's grasp of Homeric sentiment was complete'.[19] Other features also can hardly be accidental. The repeated use of moonlight; the ox-cart and Punch and Judy show amid the splendours of Rome (no.65) or the mourners at a graveside beyond the city walls (no.71); the exhausted traveller and

fig.10 John Martin, 'Manfred on the
Jungfrau', 1837, watercolour.
Birmingham Museums and Art Gallery

the dead camel by the Plain of Troy (no.63); the lovers and the funereal
gondola beneath the Bridge of Sighs (no.69) – all contribute to the
atmosphere as well as the topography of Byron's life and poetry. 'The
Castellated Rhine' (no.83), conflating several villages and fortresses into a
haunting memory of the river and its history, or 'Corinth' (no.67), its own
Acropolis claustrophobically enclosed by the surrounding mountains, are
masterly renderings of place and mood, and may be taken as perfectly
fulfilling Turner's brief. On the other hand, one anomaly stands out. It is
hard to justify the pastoral calm of his distant view of the Bernese Alps
(no.70) as a true introduction to the wild settings of *Manfred*. Strangely,
Turner's rendering partakes of none of the exhilarated sensibility of John
Martin's 'Manfred on the Jungfrau' (fig.10). Martin seems here more
Turnerian than Turner. The Sublime seems hardly to have affected
Turner's published or painted response to Byron, though it was an essen-
tial ingredient of the various productions of Byron in the London theatre
in the 1830s, and as we shall see, could well have been the emotional and
philosophical medium through which he best appreciated Byron in the last
years of his life.

Meanwhile as a footnote to the story of Murray's edition of the *Life and
Works*, it should be recorded that in 1833 Murray republished it in three
volumes, with three of Turner's illustrations, two being landscapes recycled
from Finden. The Byron industry was a self-perpetuating one, of whose
financial rewards Albemarle Street was well aware. In February 1833
Murray asked J. G. Lockhart to write an account of the Byron family, and

there were to be engraved portraits of the poet's friends. Hobhouse, who as usual disapproved, wrote hoping that 'Mr. Finden is not the engraver selected by you – for, I certainly should not permit that artist to have anything to do with me or mine after his very improper behaviour'. But the success of the illustrated *Life and Works* overshadowed any losses incurred over the *Landscape Illustrations*, and Murray had repaired relations with the Findens, encouraged by brilliant reviews. *Arnold's Magazine* spoke for many critics in finding the Byron series 'truly plates of epicurean luxuries…Turner and Finden, ye deserve canonisation'.

CONCLUSION

With the completion of his drawings for Finden and Murray, and of his painting of Ehrenbreitstein for Pye, Turner concluded his commissioned work as an illustrator of Byron. He was not involved in the Findens' other Byronic projects of the 1830s, the *Byron Gallery* and *Byron Beauties*; these turned from landscape subjects to narrative episodes or sentimental figures, for which other artists were better qualified. Thereafter Turner exhibited only three pictures with quotations from Byron (nos.37–9) and added one to a print engraved after a fourth (no.40). But it is inconceivable that he limited his consideration of Byron to these few scenes of Rome and Venice, or that he stopped thinking about him altogether in later life.

There can be no doubt that Byron remained what he had become when Turner first read *Childe Harold* – a uniquely meditative poet of travel, and the supreme commentator on post-Napoleonic Europe. Turner's professional engagements with Byron, through paintings or commissioned drawings, had all been in the arena of travel; all the subjects he had chosen or been instructed to render were foreign, from Europe or beyond. Whether or not Byron had been a contributory factor, it is striking that Turner's transformation from a relatively insular artist to one of the most widely travelled of the British Romantics took place in the years when he was reading his work. Undoubtedly Byron had contributed to Turner's mature internationalism – or at least Europeanism. He had helped him to find a context for his own observations, and to deepen his reflections on past and present. Turner may not have been as adventurous or far-reaching a traveller as Byron, but even if we leave aside his commissioned realisations of Byronic places he had never seen, we can still reconstruct many of Byron's journeys through Turner's eyes. It is impossible not to be reminded of Byron in many more of Turner's views than specifically illustrated Byron, and Turner must often have thought of Byron as he travelled in his footsteps or, in old age, looked back over his experiences abroad.

It was only in 1817 that Turner could see any part of continental Europe with Byron already in mind. But his journey to Switzerland in 1802 took him along paths the poet was to follow in 1816, and his drawings of that year map what were to become parts of the Byronic world: Avenches (no.90) with its single Roman column; the Castle of Chillon (no.91) whose famous prisoner Bonnivard, heroic champion of Liberty – 'Eternal Spirit of the chainless Mind!' – Byron later celebrated in a famous sonnet; the shores of Lake Geneva (nos.92–4), where the poet was to live in 1816 and meditate on its literary past:

> Rousseau – Voltaire – our Gibbon – and de Staël –
> Leman! these names are worthy of thy shore,
> Thy shore of names like these.

When, years later, Turner revisited Switzerland, the verses Byron had meanwhile composed must have echoed in his mind.

Had Turner made terms with Lord Elgin in 1799, he would have preceded Byron in Greece. In Athens in 1811, Byron got to know Lusieri, the artist who went instead, and Turner, for his part, was later to come into contact with others in Byron's Greek circle whose archaeological and architectural interests nourished his own. Gally Knight, whose acquaintance Byron had renewed in Greece, was the first to furnish Turner with drawings of the Temple of Aphaia at Aegina, and Turner later became a friend of Cockerell, who had excavated there. When, after his return to England in 1817, Cockerell planned a substantial publication on the temple, Turner was asked to provide finished illustrations, and his impressive view of the temple during the excavations (no.27) – not in fact published until 1860 – was apparently the only outcome of the project. In reconstructing the architecture for his earlier painting of the restored temple (no.26), Turner could also have referred to evidence from another architect, Thomas Allason, with whom he already shared mutual friends including Knight. Allason had discussed the temple with Cockerell in 1814, and was later to provide Turner with sketches of Greek subjects from which to develop his drawings for Finden and Murray. Turner was also, by the late 1820s, in contact with another architect member of that Athenian circle, Thomas Leverton Donaldson, who was Cockerell's collaborator in a supplement to Stuart's *Antiquities of Athens* published in 1830. Turner climbed Vesuvius with Donaldson in 1819, and in 1827 Donaldson supplied letterpress to a publication on Pompeii for which Turner had earlier drawn a frontispiece of the volcano. Eastlake, Turner's friend and companion during part of his second visit to Italy in 1828, had accompanied the third contributor to the supplement to the *Antiquities*, William Kinnard, on a Greek tour in 1818, and also with them was Charles Barry, to whose sketches Turner would also refer while illustrating Byron.

As we have seen, among the Greek sketches Allason supplied to Turner while he was working for Finden was one of the temple of Poseidon at Sunium (Cape Colonna). Byron visited Sunium twice, with Lusieri, Cockerell and another excavator of the Aegina marbles, the Bavarian Haller von Hallerstein, and commissioned the 'very superior German artist', Jacob Linckh, to draw this magnificent place – 'no less a haunt of painters than of pirates' – where he carved his name into a column, and which he later celebrated in his hymn to Greece and liberty in *Don Juan*:

> Place me on Sunium's marbled steep,
> Where nothing, save the waves and I,
> May hear our mutual murmurs sweep;
> There, swan-like, let me sing and die:
> A land of slaves shall ne'er be mine.

These, together with the earlier lines from *Childe Harold* –

> Tritonia's airy shrine adorns
> Colonna's cliff, and gleams along the waves

– appeared with Turner's view in Brockedon's annotated edition of Finden's *Landscape Illustrations*. Otherwise, Brockedon's notes scarcely do justice to a place which, as Turner was well aware, was hardly to be matched in richness of association. Not only had Plato supposedly held his conversations there, and Byron almost been captured by bandits, but as the notes to *Childe Harold* pointed out, Sunium was also the 'actual site' of one of the more celebrated shipwrecks in maritime literature, that recounted by William Falconer in his poem *The Shipwreck* (1762) – a work that probably made a profound impression on Turner's imagination. Turner must also have known something of the three days his friend Eastlake had spent there in 1818, with the architect George Basevi, painting 'the darkest blue sea that I suppose ever was painted'. So strongly did this particular site appeal to Turner's imagination that, alone among his Byronic subjects, he repeated it in a splendid large watercolour (no.28).

That Turner's interest in Greece was not confined to topography or architecture but extended also to history and politics had been evident from early in the century, when he had sketched a historical composition and annotated it with two alternative titles, one referring to an early declaration of freedom (no.24). The ironic comparison between ancient rights and modern slavery springs readily to mind, and is thoroughly Byronic *avant la lettre*. Turner painted subjects from Greek history throughout his life, and his pair of paintings of the temple at Aegina was the first of a long series of commentaries upon past and present. Just as it was mainly through his Greek concerns that Turner first encountered men who had known Byron, so it was these that nourished ideas that would have made him specially receptive to Byron when he came to read him.

In Switzerland and Greece, Turner had indeed anticipated Byron. The Low Countries, the Rhineland and Italy he visited with Byron already read. We know that Byron coloured his response to Waterloo. Surely, again, he must have come to mind as Turner caught the 'sea Cybele' in limpid watercolour, studied crumbling relics of the Republic's erstwhile power or seized the dazzle of the city's theatres, wineshops and fireworks that so vividly broke the gloom of the Austrian suppression. If Turner's appreciation of Greece was necessarily vicarious, in Venice he came closest to sharing Byron's own experience, and most truly understood his blend of sad reflection and excitement. In Rome also, drawing the Colosseum by night (no.103), he struck exactly the note of the doomed Manfred's recollection of standing

> within the Coliseum's wall,
> 'Midst the chief relics of almighty Rome
> ... till the place
> Became religion, and the heart ran o'er
> With silent worship of the great of old.

We may be sure that Turner's heart was similarly moved as he beheld such scenes. Byron's habit of approaching places through their history and associations, evoking their past and present condition through a few telling images, was exactly Turner's method – he had begun to demonstrate it in his own poetry before *Childe Harold* was published, and his vignettes and illustrations are only the most conspicuous of the many examples of it in his art. While he did not need to learn it from Byron, he would have recognised and remembered it in his work, and Byron's remarks on Sunium might equally stand for Turner's attitude to his own art:

> Ask the traveller what strikes him as most poetical ... the columns of Cape Colonna or the Cape itself? ... There are a thousand rocks and capes far more picturesque ... But is is the *art*, the columns, the temple, the wrecked vessels, which gives them their antique and their modern poetry, and not the spots themselves. Without them the *spots* of earth would be unnoticed and unknown.

But of course Byron offered his readers far more than a compilation of the stories and resonances familiar to his age. Indeed in recounting them he had adopted something of a pose, and looking back over his travels, once confessed that 'Hobhouse and others bored me with their learned localities'. Certainly, in the end, he paid due respect to 'the truth of *history* ... and of *place*', but throughout his published work, this gained value in pointing a moral, and here he would not always have carried Turner with him. Whether writing of the ancient liberties of Switzerland or the modern travails of Greece and Italy in *Childe Harold*, exposing the hypocrisies of English society in *The Waltz* or *Don Juan*, or condemning the cynical injustice of the post-Napoleonic order in *The Age of Bronze*, Byron had displayed an uncompromisingly radical line. In actions as well as words he had kindled the torch of freedom; while making art out of the past he gave himself enthusiastically to the present; and he died in pursuit of a better future. Turner was far less of a political animal. If he shared Byron's abstract ideals, he surely had none of his practical commitment to change. If he felt all Byron's sadness in Italy, the perception was rooted in its visible decay and did not extend, as it did with Byron, to explicit censure of the British government for 'what they have done in the South'. If he drew an Austrian sentry box in Venice (no.100), he did not insist upon it as a symbol of repression. Indeed he could be remarkably blind to the political atmosphere. In Switzerland in 1844, as a civil war approached, he hardly noticed what 'a cauldron of squabbling, political or religious, I was walking over'.

Yet if Turner did not always subscribe to Byron's political analyses, he was not necessarily unaware of them, and at least one man in his life may have come near to sharing them – Fawkes, certainly a lover of the poetry and a conservative radical who, like Byron, used his advantages of birth to proclaim the 'rights and liberties of the people'. It was surely no accident that Fawkes had acquired two of Turner's most terrible accounts of the modern world seen through Byronic eyes, his illustration to *The Giaour* portraying the captive state of Greece (p.97), and his grim watercolour of Waterloo (fig.3). Moreover, Byron's personal and professional history – as controversial and 'alternative' as his politics – may well have had an appeal to a man as privately unconventional and creatively adventurous as Turner. Radical in his own art, Turner must have been drawn to others who suffered for radicalism in their own fields; and whether or not he had noticed Byron's first critical maulings and his satirical replies, he may have identified with Byron more as attacks on his own work mounted in the last decades of his life. Each in his own way was an outsider, and it is no surprise that each made some of his most profound and affecting statements about countries other than his own.

In any case, Turner need not have shared all Byron's moral and political judgements to appreciate the completeness and complexity of his view of history and of place. Again and again, Byron had balanced opposites in ways that were bound to enlarge the vision, whether reminding his readers of the corruption and cruelty that had accompanied the splendours and supposed freedoms of the Roman Empire or the Venetian Republic, of the beauty that clung to the fading ruins of the past, or the aspirations that survived the heaviest oppression. Turner can have missed none of this, and as the author of *Fallacies of Hope* must equally have subscribed to Byron's (far from reassuring) conviction that it had all happened before and would again. Ruskin believed that Turner and Byron, with a handful of other great men of their age, had died without hope, and certainly Turner would have identified completely with Byron's longer historical perspective – the 'everlasting *to be* which *hath been*' as Byron's *Ode on Venice* described that eternal cycle wherein human ambition and greed are inevitably punished, empires and cities doomed to dust, before regeneration comes once more. It was a very eighteenth-century perspective, but in the era of Waterloo it acquired new meaning. Turner was bound to adopt Byron's response to Waterloo; like Byron, he missed none of the lessons to be drawn from the fate of Napoleon, whose shadow lay over Europe for most of his life (no.85). But unlike Byron, he lived long enough to see the inevitable change for the better that Byron had promised in his Venetian ode:

> Those momentary starts from Nature's laws
> Which like the pestilence and earthquake, smite
> But for a term, then pass, and leave the earth
> With all her seasons to repair the blight
> With a few summers, and again put forth
> Cities and generations – fair, when free –
> For, Tyranny, there blooms no bud for thee!

And it was in his own words, in verses that seem clearly marked by Byron's ideas and imagery, that Turner later celebrated the resurgence of one corner of the Continent under the civilising influence of Ludwig of Bavaria, whose Walhalla to the great men of Germany was opened in 1842:

> Who rode on thy relentless car fallacious Hope?
> He, though scathed at Ratisbon, poured on
> The tide of war o'er all thy plain, Bavare,
> Like the swollen Danube to the gates of Wien.
> But peace returns – the morning ray
> Beams on the Walhalla, reared to science and the arts,
> For men renowned, of German fatherland.

In the last canto of *Childe Harold*, Byron had brought his readers face to face with the limitations of all human achievement, save perhaps – and a doubt is left suspended – those of the arts. These alone, even when decayed, will be worthy of our respect. But Byron also asserted that in the end, Nature is the only certainty. In *Childe Harold*, Nature is often presented as a consolation, timeless and eternal, and at last the Childe turns to it gratefully. The parallel with Turner is clear, and we may wonder whether Turner could have identified a little with Harold as he read of his upbringing in crumbling Gothic halls – so similar to those he had drawn as a young topographer – of his travels, and finally of his retreat from the world of man

> To mingle with the Universe, and feel
> What I can ne'er express, yet cannot all conceal.

The final stanzas, with their hymn to the sea –

> Dark-heaving – boundless, endless and sublime,
> The image of eternity

– with its changing moods, 'calm or convulsed, in breeze, or gale, or storm', its bubbles and breakers and its 'monsters of the deep', quite remarkably forecast Turner's own concerns in whole series of painting and watercolours in his last years. Looking at these, we may be reminded, as perhaps Turner was himself if he read them in old age, of the Childe's concluding thoughts:

> but I am not now
> That which I have been – and my visions flit
> Less palpably before me.

By then, Turner could have assimilated Byron's later view of nature, that darker and more pessimistic vision of the unpredictable and irrational, of flux and change – exemplified by the shipwreck in *Don Juan* – which developed after *Childe Harold*. In his later poems and verse-dramas Byron moved from the landscape of Europe to the landscape of the mind, and from political realities to the 'politics of Paradise'. His Old Testament dramas *Heaven and Earth*, recounting the approaching Deluge, and *Cain* (1821), and his histrionic answer to Southey's attacks on *Don Juan*, *The Vision of Judgment* (1821), explore the apocalyptic Sublime to sombre or comic effect. Their imagery can be found repeated in Turner's last apocalyptic pictures. Shelley may have gone further in describing the unimaginable, and it is his *Prometheus Unbound* that is usually said to have influenced the lines Turner wrote to accompany his 'Shade and Darkness – the Evening of the Deluge' (fig.11), but the picture itself recalls much in *Heaven and Earth*. Turner connected his companion picture, 'Light and Colour … the Morning after the Deluge', with Goethe's theory of colour, and Byron also had assimilated recent thinking into *Cain*, adopting the proposition of the Frenchman Cuvier that the earth's surface had been visited by a series of revolutionary catastrophes. The body of Abel, Cain's victim, takes its place in the foreground of Turner's later painting from Revelation, 'The Angel Standing in the Sun' (fig.12), and Byron's *Cain*, which draws to a close with the appearance of the Angel of the Lord, might be added to the varied stimuli for that remarkable picture. If Turner's 'Angel' was indeed, as some have thought, a triumphant repudiation of the painter's many critics, it could have reminded him of Byron's *Vision of Judgment*, in which the Archangel Michael, a 'beautiful and mighty Thing of Light', bursts forth to help examine King George III for admission to Heaven, before being distracted – as Byron had recently been – by the irritating intrusion of Southey. The *Vision* is indeed a memorable work, richly comic and a superb put-down. In his independence of spirit and

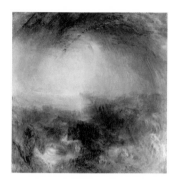

fig.11 'Shade and Darkness – the Evening of the Deluge', exh.1843, oil on canvas (B&J 404). *Tate Gallery* (N00531)

fig.12 'The Angel Standing in the Sun', exh. 1846, oil on canvas (B&J 425). *Tate Gallery* (N00550)

artistic integrity, as well as in his ideas, Byron was a shining inspiration in a world of compromise. Turner, surely, was moved by the artist as well as by the art; and not least by his jokes.

If, in the last decades of his life, Turner was acutely aware of Byron's views of nature, history and society, and bound on many occasions to filter his own experience through Byronic recollection, it must also be remembered that a whole generation now approached Byron through Turner. Although it was John Martin, rather than Turner, whose apocalyptic visions translated more readily into stage designs for the production of Byron's dramas on the London stage, Academy visitors, readers of Moore's *Life and Works* and Finden's *Landscape Illustrations*, and purchasers of the large plates engraved after 'Waterloo' (no.35), 'Ehrenbreitstein' (p.93), 'Childe Harold's Pilgrimage' (no.36) or 'St Mark's Place, Venice' (no.40) read Byron or traced his life with Turner's images stamped indelibly on their minds. No doubt there were those who missed the stories and characters – Childe Harold himself, Manfred or the Giaour. Yet it is precisely their absence that enabled Turner to enter more deeply into Byron's mental and physical landscape, and to create pictures that are largely immune to changing tastes and values. Today they remain what they were for his contemporaries – a definitive panorama of the Byronic world.

NOTES

1. Turner to John Britton, November 1811, in J. Gage, *Collected Correspondence of J.M.W. Turner*, 1980, p.51, no.43
2. A. Wilton, *Turner Abroad*, 1982, p.25
3. G.H. Hamilton, 'Eugène Delacroix and Lord Byron', *Gazette des Beaux Arts*, XXIII, 1943, pp.99–110; 'Hamlet or Childe Harold? Delacroix and Byron', *ibid.*, XXVI, 1944, pp.336–66; 'Delacroix, Byron and the English Illustrators', *ibid.*, XXXVI, 1949, pp.261–78. See more recently Lee Johnson, 'Delacroix and the *Bride of Abydos*', *Burlington Magazine*, CCIX, 1972, pp.579–85, and P. Joannides, 'Colin, Delacroix, Byron and the Greek War of Independence', ibid., CXXV, 1983, pp.495–500.
4. F. Berry, 'The Poet of Childe Harold', in *Byron, A Symposium*, ed. J.D. Jump, 1975, pp.35–51
5. Byron to J. Murray, 4 September 1817, 14 July 1820, 31 August 1820, in *The Works of Lord Byron: Letters and Journals*, ed. Prothero, 1906 IV, pp.164, 219; V, p.68
6. F. Owen and D.B. Brown, *Collector of Genius: A Life of Sir George Beaumont*, 1988, pp.139–40
7. A. Wilton, with Rosalind Mallord Turner, *Painting and Poetry: Turner's Verse Book and his Work of 1804–1812*, 1990, pp.101–5, 170–6
8. J. Gage, 'Turner and the Greek Spirit', *Turner Studies*, vol.I, no.2 1981, pp.14–25
9. R. Christiansen, *Romantic Affinities: Portraits from an Age, 1780–1830*, 1988, p.197
10. W. Hazlitt in *The Yellow Dwarf*, 1818, in *Byron: The Critical Heritage*, ed. A. Rutherford, 1970, p.133
11. W. Scott in *Quarterly Review*, in Rutherford 1970, p.145
12. Hazlitt, in Rutherford 1970, p.133
13. R. Altick, *Paintings from Books. Art and Literature in Britain, 1760–1900*, Columbus, Ohio 1985, p.438
14. *The Works of John Ruskin*, ed. E.T. Cook and A. Wedderburn, XIII, 1904, pp.140–5
15. Ibid., VII, p.431
16. M. Foot, *The Politics of Paradise: A Vindication of Byron*, 1988, p.208
17. All correspondence transcribed here is quoted by kind permission of John Murray Ltd.
18. *The Works of John Ruskin*, XIII, p.445
19. Ibid., pp.446–7

35 **The Field of Waterloo** RA 1818
  1475 × 2390 (58 × 94)

36 **Childe Harold's Pilgrimage – Italy** RA 1832
  1420 × 2480 (56 × 97¾)

Page 97 *Illustration to 'The Giaour':*
The Acropolis of Athens 1822
187 × 127 (7^1/$_{16}$ × 5^5/$_6$)

19 Sir Charles Lock Eastlake
Lord Byron's 'Dream' RA 1829
1181 × 1708 (46 × 67^1/$_4$)

27 **The Temple of Aphaia at Aegina,
during Excavations** *c.*1825
267 × 432 (11⅝ × 17⁵⁄₁₆)

28 **The Temple of Poseidon at Sunium
(Cape Colonna)** *c.*1834
375 × 584 (14¾ × 23)

Page 93 **The Bright Stone of Honour (Ehrenbreitstein),
and Tomb of Marceau, from Byron's 'Childe Harold'** RA 1835
930 × 1230 (36⅝ × 48⁷⁄₁₆)

38 **Venice, the Bridge of Sighs** RA 1840
610 × 915 (24 × 36)

37 **Modern Rome – Campo Vaccino** RA 1839
902 × 1220 (35½ × 48)

Ex-cat. **Approach to Venice** RA 1844
oil on canvas 623 × 940 (24½ × 37)
National Gallery of Art, Washington D.C.;
Andrew W. Mellon Collection (B&J 412) (see no.39)

92 **Lausanne and Lake Geneva** 1841
236 × 334 (9⁵/₁₆ × 13³/₁₆)

96 **Venice: Looking East from the
Giudecca – Early Morning** 1819
222 × 287 (8³/₄ × 11³/₈)

99 **Venice, the Arsenal** *c.*1840
243 × 308 (9⅝ × 12½)

85 **War. The Exile and the Rock Limpet** RA 1842
795 × 795 (31¼ × 31¼)

103 **The Colosseum by Moonlight** 1819
232 × 369 (9¹⁄₈ × 14³⁄₈)

102 **Rome: The Forum with a Rainbow** 1819
229 × 366 (9¹⁄₈ × 14³⁄₄)

CATALOGUE

CATALOGUE NOTE

Unless otherwise stated, works are by J.M.W. Turner. Measurements are given in millimetres, followed by inches in brackets, height before width. Items illustrated in colour are marked with an asterisk.

Abbreviations

B&J   Martin Butlin and Evelyn Joll, *The Paintings of J.M.W. Turner*, 2 vols., revised ed. 1984

R   W.G. Rawlinson, *The Engraved Work of J.M.W. Turner, R.A.*, 2 vols., 1908 and 1913

RA   Exhibited at the Royal Academy

TB   A.J. Finberg, *A Complete Inventory of the Drawings of the Turner Bequest*, 2 vols., 1909

W   Andrew Wilton, *The Life and Work of J.M.W. Turner*, 1979 (catalogue of watercolours)

For other published material which is abbreviated in the text, see Bibliography.

IMAGES OF THE POET: EARLY PORTRAITS AND ILLUSTRATIONS OF BYRON

Contemporary portraits of Byron, whether from the life or imaginary, and many posthumous images, present not only an individual but a type – a romantic wanderer and a personification of ideas of personal, political or moral freedom. The relationship between the poet and his poetic heroes was recognised from the first, and Sanders's portrait (no.1) is an extraordinary premonition of the image of Byron that reached a climax in Eastlake's 'Byron's "Dream"' (no.19), which showed the poet in contemplation in a landscape from Greece or the eastern Mediterranean – the area particularly associated with him not only by his writings, but also by his death in the cause of Greek independence in 1824. Eastlake was one of the two or three most enthusiastic Byronists among Turner's friends, and probably helped to introduce him to Byron's work; fittingly, he probably based the architectural background of his picture on a work by Turner and Turner may later have prepared another very Byronic subject (no.28) to be engraved as a companion to a print after the Eastlake.

Turner could also have been introduced to Byron's

work by mutual friends like Samuel Rogers, although his keen interest in poetry would have led him to it independently. Byron was controversial from the first and Turner was meanwhile deeply concerned with writing poetry himself, with the nature of poetic inspiration, and with the critical climate. Besides friends, Turner and Byron shared critics in common, the most prominent being Sir George Beaumont. Both reacted in comic terms to attacks by lesser men. Whether knowingly or not, Turner's 'The Garreteer's Petition' (no.6) is a skit on the very sorts of poets Byron had attacked in his first notable work, *English Bards and Scotch Reviewers*.

GEORGE SANDERS (1774–1846)

1   **Lord Byron and a Companion, with a Boat**
c.1807
Oil on canvas
1130 × 892 (44^{1}/$_{2}$ × 35^{1}/$_{8}$)
Her Majesty the Queen

Begun in 1807, this remarkable portrait may have drawn its powerful narrative elements from Byron's early passion for travel, and particularly from his frustrated plan to sail to the Hebrides – and if conditions allowed as far as Iceland – that same year. Byron is shown on a lonely and mountainous shore, perhaps suggestive of the Western Isles, and his young companion is thought to be Robert Rushton, the son of one of his Newstead tenants who joined him on his travels in 1809. The portrait is a remarkable anticipation of the wandering poet and hero of

Childe Harold, and of Harold's faithful page. The painter, in Byron's words a 'noted limner', had arrived in London from Edinburgh in 1805 and built up a fashionable practice as portraitist and miniaturist in Vigo Street. Byron paid 250 guineas for the portrait and concluded it 'does not *flatter* me ... but the subject is a bad one'. By July 1810 it had been sent to his mother at Newstead; she thought 'the countenance is *angelic* and the finest I ever saw ... very like'. Having subsequently fallen for a time into the care of John Murray, it was given to Byron's friend Hobhouse, in whose collection it was when engraved by William Finden for Moore's *Life* of the poet (1830); the print announces that Byron is shown aged nineteen, while the engraving made by Edward Finden in 1834 states the original to have been painted in 1807. For William Finden's print and its important repercussions, see Introduction and no.41.

ATTRIBUTED TO RUDOLF (RIDOLFO) SCHADOW
(1786–1822)

2 **Byron**
White marble, oval
218 × 163 (8⁹/₁₆ × 6⁷/₁₆)
Inscribed on base of neck 'BYRON. ROM.'
Private Collection

Byron visited Rome with Hobhouse between 29 April and 20 May 1817. His impressions of its ruins, works of art, history and legends under Hobhouse's tutelage formed the substance of the fourth and last canto of *Childe Harold,* which he dedicated to his friend. While in Rome, Byron sat to the celebrated Danish sculptor Bertel Thorvaldsen for a bust commissioned by Hobhouse for himself; the original clay bust is in the Thorvaldsen Museum, Copenhagen, and marble versions are in the Royal Collection and elsewhere. Hobhouse had wished Byron to be portrayed wearing a laurel wreath, but the poet had protested: 'I won't have my head garnished like a Christmas pie with holly – or a cod's head and fennel, or whatever the damned weed is they strew round it. I wonder you should want me to be such a mountebank' (20 June 1817). In fact the relief published here, which was discovered by Dr Andrew Ciechanowiecki in Paris in 1986 and has not previously been exhibited or described, is the only portrait of Byron with a laurel wreath. It presents a less solemn (and more fleshy) image of Byron than Thorvaldsen's bust, and is different in the execution of details, especially of the hair. For these reasons it cannot be a copy of the profile of Thorvaldsen's bust, but as Byron is shown with his characteristic lobeless ear, the sculptor must have had access either to the sitter or to a convincing *ad vivum* portrait. The inscription indicates that the relief was executed in Rome by a German or Danish sculptor, 'Rom' being the city's name in both languages, but as Byron was busy sightseeing during his three weeks there, it is unlikely that he would have given sittings to another sculptor. The attribution to the German Rudolf (Ridolfo) Schadow, first proposed by Joanna Barnes on stylistic grounds, is therefore an attractive one as he was a pupil of Thorvaldsen and remained on close terms with him. He could have made this relief, or a sketch model for it, while Byron was sitting to Thorvaldsen. He remained in Rome until his death in 1822. On the other Byronic sculpture see J. Kenworthy-Browne, 'Byron Portrayed', *Antique Collector,* July 1974. Gerald Burdon has given invaluable help in describing this new example.

JOHN LINNELL (1792–1882)

3 **Samuel Rogers**
Oil on wood
394 × 349 (15½ × 13¾)
N05117

Samuel Rogers (1763–1855), banker, poet and wit, guided Byron through the literary and political circles of London when Byron first arrived in the capital in 1811. Byron had already dealt kindly with Rogers' early poem *The Pleasures of Memory* (1792) in his own early work, *English Bards and Scotch Reviewers* (1809), and remained a grateful and affectionate friend until rumours of Rogers's gossip about him reached him in Italy. Rogers, despite his barbed tongue, remained fond of Byron and after his death did him full honour in the 'Bologna' section of his poem, *Italy:*

> Yes, BYRON, thou art gone,
> Gone like a star thro' the firmament
> Shot and was lost, in its eccentric course
> Dazzling, perplexing. Yet thy heart, methinks,
> Was generous, noble …

Rogers was also a friend of Turner, and it was the huge success of Turner's vignette illustrations to *Italy*, commissioned by the poet for a special edition published in 1830, that helped to inspire other editions of modern authors illustrated by Turner – among them Murray's popular edition of Moore's *Life and Works* of Byron (no.59).

CHARLES MOTTRAM (1807–1876)
AFTER JOHN DOYLE (1797–1868)

4 **Samuel Rogers at his Breakfast Table**
Engraving and mezzotint
580 × 866 (23 × 34) on wove paper 658 × 902
(26 × 35½); plate mark 642 × 876 (25¼ × 34½)
Engraved inscriptions: 'Pedestal carved by Sir Francis Chantrey R.A.' below image bottom left, 'Anno 1815' below image near centre, 'Charles Mottram' below image bottom right, and, from left to right, facsimile signatures of the sitters
T04907

Rogers was famous for his breakfast parties at his town house, 22 St James's Place, which brought together leading figures in politics, the arts and the professions. Both Turner and Byron were entertained there, and this print shows them attending on the same occasion, supposedly in 1815. In fact this particular party is imaginary, representing a gathering of all Rogers's most distinguished friends, but it portrays the social circle in which Turner and Byron could have met, if at all.

Rogers himself is seated in the foreground, his face turned in profile, with Byron beside him; Turner appears on the right. Among the other guests are Walter Scott, Thomas Moore, Wordsworth, Southey, Coleridge and Campbell. John Doyle, who drew this remarkable assembly, later turned to the production of caricature lithographs, adopting the initials 'H.B.'.

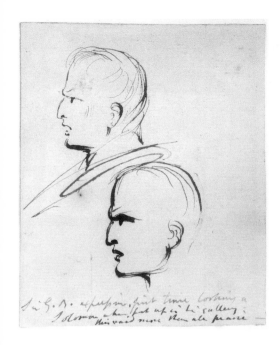

BENJAMIN ROBERT HAYDON (1786–1846)

5   **Sir George Beaumont** 1814
Pen and ink
121 × 98 (4½ × 3¹⁵/₁₆)
Inscribed: 'Sir G.B. expression first time looking at
Solomon when put up in his gallery: this said more
than all praise'
A00192

Drawn here while inspecting Haydon's 'Judgement of Solomon' at the British Institution in 1814, Beaumont was the most influential connoisseur and patron of painting and poetry in the first two decades of the century. He intensely disliked Turner's work, rallying a critical campaign against it, and took only a distant and disapproving interest in Byron. With his wife, he was a devoted friend and generous patron of the Lake Poets whom Byron satirised in his first popular and conspicuous poem, *English Bards and Scotch Reviewers* (1809), and was also the protector of William Lisle Bowles, whose sanctimonious and moralistic edition of Alexander Pope (1806) Byron attacked in a published letter to John Murray in 1821. Turner may well have been encouraged and amused by Byron's robust replies to his critics – indeed it may have been these that first brought Byron to his attention – at a time when he was himself under heavy attack from Beaumont. The Beaumonts entertained Byron occasionally – with Wordsworth in 1812 and again with Rogers and Walter Scott in 1815 – but Lady Beaumont considered his mind 'near derangement' and lamented his 'want of more lastingly devout principle'. Byron repaid the compliment by casting the Beaumonts as Sir George and Lady Bluemont in his 'literary eclogue' on blue-stocking society, *The Blues* (1820; published in *The Liberal*, 1823).

6   **The Garreteer's Petition** RA 1809
Oil on mahogany panel
550 × 790 (21³/₄ × 31¹/₈)
B&J 100
N00482

Turner exhibited this satirical portrait of a distressed poet in a gloomy garret, striking a heroic pose as he struggles to rally his failing inspiration, with lines of his own verse:

> Aid me, ye Powers! O bid my thoughts to roll
> In quick succession, animate my soul;
> Descend my Muse, and every thought refine,
> And finish well my long, my *long-sought* line.

The quotation was condensed from a longer draft, sketched with the drawing for this picture, probably made the previous year, also in the Turner Bequest (D08256). Without identifying himself with this troubled poetaster, Turner has presented a clear picture of ambition and incompetence combined; the print of Mount Parnassus on the wall indicates the garreteer's doomed aspirations. Another drawing in the Bequest of the same date and uniform in style (D08257) portrays a painter busy over a derivative canvas, surrounded by old masters to crib from; here too Turner uses the medium of comic genre to address serious questions about the nature of creativity. Artistic ineptitude had been a favourite butt of the Augustan poets, and their methods had recently been applied in the context of the contemporary art world by Turner's fellow painter Martin Archer Shee in his poem *Rhymes on Art*, published with some success in 1806 and expanded as *Elements of Art* in 1809. Shee's volume was well received by Byron, and together with the more important influence of the Augustans themselves – above all Alexander Pope – it contributed to the genesis of Byron's brilliantly witty parody of his own early critics, *English Bards and Scotch Reviewers*, published in 1809. The appearance of Turner's picture of an incompetent and bombastic poet in the same year as Byron's attack on just such people may be no more than a remarkable coincidence, but at the very least it indicates a similar cast of mind and a similar inspiration.

8 **Landscape Annual 1831: The Tourist in Italy**
By Thomas Roscoe. Illustrated from Drawings by S. Prout, Esq. F.S.A.
London, 1831
93 × 142 ($3^{11}/_{16}$ × $5^{5}/_{8}$)
Open at pp.76–7: 'Mocenigo Palace, Venice'
Dr Jan Piggott

Byron moved into the Palazzo Mocenigo before 1 June 1818, having secured it at the very economical rent of 200 louis a year. Robert Wallis's engraving after Prout was published in the *Landscape Annual* opposite an essay on 'Lord Byron's Palace'. Prefaced with a quotation from *Childe Harold* IV, it tells nothing of the palace, and (though very subjectively) a certain amount of the poet's mental condition – 'The prospect of dominion subdued, a high spirit humbled, of splendour tarnished, of palaces sinking into ruins, was but too faithfully in accordance with the dark and mournful mind which the poet bore within him'. Then it plunges into an account of 'the dissipations of Lord Byron's Venetian life', and concludes with a firm rebuke for a career misspent in a selfish pursuit of pleasure and ambition.

Although produced in 1831, at the height of anti-Byron reaction, Roscoe's volume is nevertheless suffused with the Byronic spirit. Quotations from Byron are everywhere, and the poet's own mingled sensations of melancholy and pleasure, his appreciation of the beauty in decay and the corruption that coexists with valour and nobility even at the zenith of a nation's power, are constantly reflected in the text. 'Rome and Venice', the introduction reminded the reader, 'are not places to be passed over in a season. Mirrors of wisdom to future ages – as full of moral doctrine as of monuments of mightier days – the utter extremes of human power and weakness are typified in their history and their doom'. For all Roscoe's distaste for Byron's personal life, his readers could hardly find a better primer to the Byronic mind. Turner owned a copy.

JAMES HOLLAND (1799–1870)
7 **Byron by the Rialto Bridge, Venice**
Watercolour on toned paper, vignette
377 × 249 ($14^{13}/_{16}$ × $9^{13}/_{16}$)
Inscribed: 'Ponte di Rialto Venezia'
Lionel Lambourne

Like Lake Price's watercolour of Byron in his Venetian *salone* (no.9), Holland's vignette is a romanticised image, designed to take advantage of the Byronic mythology, in which the poet's period of residence in Venice, on and off between 1817 and 1820, occupied a particularly compelling place on account both of its important literary progeny – including the first canto of *Don Juan* – and the rumours of his dissipated life in the city. Holland's likeness is taken at second hand, probably from Charles Turner's mezzotint after Richard Westall's portrait. The setting is fanciful, although we may suppose Byron on a balcony of the Palazzo Mocenigo, which stands not far from the Rialto.

WILLIAM LAKE PRICE (1810–1891)

9 **Byron in the Palazzo Mocenigo** 1839
Watercolour and bodycolour
343 × 483 (13½ × 19)
Private Collection

Price was taught watercolour painting and architectural drawing by Augustus Charles Pugin. This elaborate watercolour, one of many romanticised posthumous images of Byron, shows him in the drawing room of the Palazzo Mocenigo, succumbing to poetic vapours at his desk. The poet's pose is derived from a portrait by Richard Westall. It was reproduced in colour lithograph by Price himself.

GEORGE JONES (1786–1869)

10 **The Youth of Childe Harold**
Pencil
310 × 265 (12⅜ × 10¹³/₁₆)
Signed in Greek letters at right of image, inscribed 'Canto I. 1.2 Childe Harold' below image
bottom right
Private Collection

The first two cantos of *Childe Harold's Pilgrimage* were published on 10 March 1812, and in further editions that year. This and the following drawings illustrating *Childe Harold* belong to a series of fifteen made by Jones very soon after the poem was published; four are dated 1812, and one 1813. A set of subjects from *The Giaour* (for example nos.13 and 14) is uniform in style and must likewise date from soon after the publication of the poem in 1813. While Jones was among the very first to seize upon the pictorial possibilities of Byron's poetry, he cannot be said to have exploited them very thoroughly. His designs reveal little sense of the atmosphere and settings of the poems, and scarcely even attempt appropriate costume and detail, depending instead on established conventions of literary illustration. His subjects from *Childe Harold* are in many cases intended to reveal the psychology of the hero, and are thus very interesting as early investigations of a temperament which, on account of its evident relation to that of its creator, fascinated and tantalised a generation of readers, but their effect is somewhat dissipated by the stylistic language. Here, Jones has reduced the indulgences of the Childe's jaded and disaffected youth (actually spent in Gothic halls) to a rather tame neoclassical orgy. The drawing illustrates lines from the second stanza:

> Ah me! in sooth he was a shameless wight,
> Sore given to revel and ungodly glee;
> Few earthly things found favour in his sight
> Save concubines and carnal companie,
> And flaunting wassailers of high and low degree.

Gerald Burdon has kindly assisted in describing Jones's drawings.

GEORGE JONES (1786–1869)

11 **The Maid of Saragossa**
Pencil
325 × 270 (12³⁄₄ × 10⁵⁄₈)
Inscribed 'To face p.36, C.1, S. 50, 57' below image
bottom right
Private Collection

In *Childe Harold* i.lvi Byron tells the story of the heroic
Maid of Saragossa who, at the siege of the city during the
Spanish rising against the French occupation in 1808, took
over her dead husband's cannon and fired it straight at an
advancing French column. The Spanish resistance to the
French, epitomised by this episode, was a focus for libertarian and anti-Napoleonic feeling in England. Byron,
who visited Spain on his first tour abroad, was among the
first to celebrate the Maid in literature, and added in his
notes to the poem that 'When the author was at Seville,
she walked daily on the Prado, decorated with medals and
orders, by command of the Junta'. Jones's drawing is one
of the earliest renderings of the heroine, and perhaps the
first to take account of Byron's lines:

> Her lover sinks – she sheds no ill-time tear;
> Her chief is slain – she fills his fatal post;
> Her fellows fell – she checks their base career;
> The foe retires – she heads the sallying host:
> Who can appease her like a lover's ghost?

As a historical and battle painter who had served in the
Peninsular Army from 1811, Jones must have found this
documentary episode particularly affecting.

GEORGE JONES (1786–1869)

12 **Childe Harold alone in the Crowd** 1812
Pencil
310 × 265 (12³⁄₈ × 10¹³⁄₁₆)
Signed in Greek letters and dated 1812, bottom
left of image, inscribed 'Can 2 S 26' below image
bottom right
Private Collection

The date confirms that Jones's were indeed among the
very first illustrations to *Childe Harold*, made the same year
as the first two cantos were published. Here he has chosen to explore the Childe's meditation on the true nature
of solitude in the second canto, xxvi; it is not to be found
in lonely contemplation of Nature, but within the self, even
in the busiest places:

> But midst the crowd, the hum, the shock of men,
> To hear, to see, to feel, and to possess,
> And roam along, the world's tired denizen,
> With none who bless us, none whom we can bless
> …
> This is to be alone – This, this is Solitude!

GEORGE JONES (1786–1869)

13 Illustration to 'The Giaour': 'He who hath bent him o'er the dead'
Pencil
318 × 270 (12³/₄ × 10⁵/₈)
Signed in Greek letters and dated 1813, below image bottom left, and inscribed 'Giaour, line 68, He who hath bent him o'er the dead' on verso
Private Collection

Seven editions of *The Giaour* appeared in 1813, the first on 5 June. Seven of the series of twelve drawings by Jones to which nos.13 and 14 belong are dated that year. Jones seems to have been impressed by the Greek settings of both this poem and *Childe Harold,* and may have shared Byron's philhellene sentiments. Here Jones has taken the striking and justly famous passage in which Byron uses a newly dead corpse as a metaphor for the present state of Greece under Turkish subjugation:

> He who hath bent him o'er the dead
> Ere the first day of death is fled,
> He still might doubt the tyrant's power,
> So fair – so calm – so softly seal'd
> The first – last look – by death reveal'd!
> …
> Such is the aspect of this shore –
> T'is Greece – but living Greece no more!

It is interesting to compare Jones's rendering with Turner's, made for Walter Fawkes a few years later (p.97) in which the meaning is made far clearer and more poignant by the placing of the figures before the Acropolis.

GEORGE JONES (1786–1869)

14 Monkir and Nekir with the Body of Hassan on their Scythe
Pencil
320 × 167 (12⁷/₁₆ × 10¹/₂)
Signed in Greek letters and dated 1813, and inscribed '7' bottom right of image
Private Collection

The exotic possibilities of Byron's Oriental tales attracted numerous artists. Jones's drawing depicts one of the most gruesome passages in *The Giaour,* in which the body of Hassan, whom the Giaour has killed to avenge the death of his lover Leila, is impaled on the scythe born by the two angels of death:

> But thou, false Infidel! shalt writhe
> Beneath avenging Monkir's scythe;
> And from its torment 'scape alone
> To wander round lost Eblis' throne;
> And fire unquench'd, unquenchable,
> Around, within, thy heart shall dwell.

The notes to the poem explain that 'Monkir and Nekir are the inquisitors of the dead, before whom the corpse undergoes a slight noviciate and preparatory training for damnation. If the answers are none of the clearest, he is hauled up with a scythe and thumped down with a red-hot mace till properly seasoned … The office of these angels is no sinecure, there are but two, and … their hands are always full'. Eblis, we are further informed, is 'the Oriental Prince of Darkness'. Jones's interpretation of the purgatorial sufferings of Byron's Infidel is based mainly on the late eighteenth-century vocabulary of illustrations to Milton, exemplified by Fuseli.

JOHANN HEINRICH FUSELI (1741–1825)

15 **Conrad Liberates Gulnare**
Black chalk
187 × 177 (7⁵⁄₁₆ × 7)
Inscribed bottom right: 'P.H. Sep.tr 6.15'
Courtauld Institute Galleries, London (Witt Collection)

Fuseli was among the first painters to take a serious interest in Byron, avidly buying everything he wrote on its
first publication; he was also among the few who in
their turn attracted the poet's favourable attention, and on
22 March 1814 Byron recorded in his journal that 'The
Princess of Wales had requested Fuseli to paint from "The
Corsair", – leaving to him the choice of any passage for
the subject' (Moore, *Life*, II, p.17). No painting is known
today, but two drawings, including this example, are
recorded, both showing the pirate chief Conrad carrying
Gulnare from the harem of his enemy the Turkish Pasha
Seyd, Fuseli having selected the lines from canto II.v:

> But who is she? whom Conrad's arms convey
> From reeking pile and combat's wreck away –
> Who but the lover of him he dooms to bleed?
> The Harem queen – but still the slave of Seyd!

Byron's Oriental tales were for some years the most
popular sources for illustrators seeking exotic or romantic
interest; Fuseli's interpretation is somewhat different from
the next generation's in avoiding the temptation to costume drama and retaining instead a neo-classical coolness
and severity.

THOMAS STOTHARD (1755–1834)

16 **Selim Discovered with Zuleika by Giaffir and
his Men** *c.*1814
Watercolour
234 × 180 (9½ × 7¹⁄₁₆)
Board of Trustees of the Victoria and Albert Museum, London

An illustration to *The Bride of Abydos*, II.xxi–xxii. Stothard,
among the most prolific illustrators of his time, was one of
the first to illustrate Byron commercially. During the second decade of the century he designed twelve plates for
John Murray which certainly appeared in the collected
editions of Byron's *Works* published in 1815 and 1818, although there is some evidence that they could have
appeared earlier; Robert Balmanno's collection of prints
after Stothard in the British Museum Print Room includes
twelve proofs said to be 'For John Murray 1814' (#1660 *et
seq.*) and Stothard's biographer A.C. Coxhead claimed
some were first produced in 1813 (see Shelley M. Bennett,
*Thomas Stothard: The Mechanisms of Art Patronage in England
circa 1800*, University of Missouri Press, Columbia 1988,
pp.80–1). Like most early illustrators of Byron, Stothard
chose exotic or sentimental figure subjects, strongly
favouring the Oriental tales. *The Bride of Abydos*, first published in December 1813, tells the tragic story of Zuleika,
whose marriage, arranged by her father, the Pasha Giaffir,
is much resented by her brother Selim. In a grotto by the
Hellespont, Selim – a brooding and quintessentially Byronic figure – reveals that he is not her brother but her
cousin, and a pirate chief whose own father had been
murdered by Giaffir. Declaring his love for Zuleika, Selim
prepares to flee with her, but – at the moment depicted
by Stothard – Giaffir's men burst in and shoot him as he
tries to escape in a boat. Zuleika dies of a broken heart.

The Prisoner of Chillon.

JOHN VARLEY (1778–1842)

17 **Illustration to 'The Bride of Abydos'**
Watercolour
157 × 216 (6½ × 8½)
Board of Trustees of the Victoria and Albert Museum, London

Varley was keenly interested in Byron, and in 1821, having received from the Water-Colour Society the annual premium given 'to induce the artist to undertake a work of elaborate composition for the ensuing exhibition', produced 'A Scene from the *Bride of Abydos'*. This – which according to the Redgraves' rather cutting account was 'important at least as to size' (*A Century of Painters*, 1866, p.496) – was evidently one of Varley's epic exhibition machines in which he gave rein to his love for architectural fantasy or historical reconstruction. The subject was 'within the place of a thousand tombs', from the final passage (II.xxviii) in which Byron describes Zuleika's resting place. This small watercolour is presumably a study for the larger work.

GEORGE CRUIKSHANK (1792–1878)

18 **Illustrations of Lord Byron**
Open at 'The Prisoner of Chillon'
Wood engraving, vignette
214 × 127 (8⁷⁄₁₆ × 5)
Dr Jan Piggott

Cruikshank's series of Byron subjects, some of which were first published by J. Robins and Co., London, in 1824, are among the artist's earlier works as a book illustrator. They were issued again in George Clinton's *Memoirs of the Life and Writings of Lord Byron*, which appeared in parts between 30 June and 16 July 1825, and in bound copies published by Robins in 1826 (see G.W. Reid, *A Descriptive Catalogue of the Work of George Cruikshank*, 1871, I, pp.233–5, nos.3304–42). They are somewhat perfunctory renderings in outline, Cruikshank's lively draughtsmanship having suffered in transfer to the woodblock. The subjects are typical of the first phase of Byron illustration – romantic, dramatic, or humorous, with an emphasis on the exotic or grotesque. *The Prisoner of Chillon* was for a long time the most popular of Byron's shorter poems as a subject for illustration, not least because, in its depiction of the sufferings of the captive Bonnivard, it echoed the famous Dante subject – memorably painted by Reynolds – of Ugolino in the Tower (see D. Altick, *Paintings from Books: Art and Literature in Britain, 1760–1900*, Columbus, Ohio 1985, p.442).

SIR CHARLES LOCK EASTLAKE (1793–1865)

19 **Lord Byron's 'Dream'*** 1827 RA 1829
Oil on canvas
1181 × 1708 (46 × 67¼)
N00898

Painted in Rome from 1827, Eastlake's picture offers a definitive image of a melancholy or reflective wanderer in distant lands. The subject is clearly Byron himself, as it is also in Byron's poem *The Dream* (1816), lines from the fourth stanza of which accompanied the picture when shown at the Academy:

> and in the last he lay
> Reposing from the noontide sultriness,
> Couch'd among fallen columns, in the shade
> Of ruin'd walls that had survived the names
> Of those who rear'd them, by his sleeping side
> Stood camels grazing, and some goodly steeds
> Were fasten'd near a fountain; and a man
> Clad in a flowing garb did watch a while,
> While many of his tribe slumbered around.

This stanza was admired by Walter Scott as a 'perfect Eastern picture'.

Eastlake had begun to assemble ideas and sketches for the picture in Naples in 1824, and finished it in Rome for his friend the Earl of Leven and Melville. Turner had no doubt watched its progress during his visits to Eastlake in Rome in 1828, and the following year wrote to report its arrival in the Academy (Gage, *Correspondence*, no.149). Eastlake seems to have based the architectural background on Turner's treatment of the ruined temple of Aphaia at Aegina in 'View of the Temple of Jupiter Panellenius, in the Island of Aegina, … the Acropolis of Athens in the Distance' (1814 or 1816: the Duke of Northumberland). In turn Eastlake's vivid realisation of a Byronic landscape perhaps helped to inspire Turner's 'Childe Harold's Pilgrimage' (no.36).

Eastlake's picture was engraved in 1834 by J.T. Willmore. This print was Willmore's first large plate. See no.

28 for Turner's large watercolour of Sunium, and a suggestion that this was intended to be engraved as a companion plate.

SIR CHARLES LOCK EASTLAKE (1793–1865)

20 **Haidée, a Greek Girl** 1827 RA 1831
Oil on canvas
635 × 508 (25 × 20)
N00398

Exhibited to illustrate the lines from *Don Juan*, II.cxviii

> Her brow was white and low, her cheek's pure dye
> Like twilight rosy still with the set sun;
> Short upper lip – sweet lips! that make us sigh
> Ever to have seen such; for she was one
> Fit for the model of a statuary.

Painted for Eastlake's friend and patron Jeremiah Harman, 'Haidée' personified the philhellenic spirit of its time and all a Northerner's yearning for the warmth and sensuality of the South. Eastlake adopted a warm tonality to match Byron's description and admitted, 'she would not do in Somerset House among the "pale unripened beauties of the North" – who, by-the-by, are much paler and whiter in English pictures than in nature'. The painter had felt some reluctance to refer to such a controversial, even disreputable poem as *Don Juan* – and indeed Haidée is therein cast as the epitome of sexual and spiritual freedom, dwelling on an island that is literally and metaphorically a lost ideal. He overcame his scruples, however, recognising that no poem or character better expressed the image of remote and transient beauty he sought in the picture. Like 'Lord Byron's "Dream"' (no.19), 'Haidée' was painted in Rome – where Turner doubtless saw it on the easel – and exhibited later in London, where the Duke of Wellington declared it 'the best picture in the Exhibition'.

APPROACHING BYRON: GREECE AND HISTORIC EUROPE

From his youth Turner was deeply interested in the history and antiquities of Greece. These concerns were inspired first by his interest in architecture, and by his need to assemble suitable material for paintings of historic landscape, and it was in large part through his exploration of Greek subjects that Turner developed the insights into the historic and moral resonance of landscape that so greatly distinguished his own art, and made him profoundly receptive to Byron's. In 1799 Turner was invited by Lord Elgin to accompany him on his archaeological tour of the East, and had he accepted, he would have preceded Byron to Athens. In fact his Greek material was gathered from secondary sources, from extensive reading and from travellers like Henry Gally Knight who had known Byron in Greece or who, like the philhellene Eastlake, had followed in his footsteps. It was another friend, Walter Fawkes, who about 1822 commissioned Turner's first illustration to Byron in watercolour, a view of the Acropolis depicting a passage in *The Giaour.* The Greek subjects Turner subsequently made to illustrate Byron's life and works for publication were similarly compiled from secondary sources. So too were Turner's illustrations to James Hakewill's volume on Italy (1819), one of which was published near an appropriate quotation from Byron – the first time that the close affinity between Turner's imaginative conception of place and Byron's poetry was recognised in a book, although Turner had already published verses from Byron in the Royal Academy catalogue the previous year. The poet himself acquired a copy of Hakewill's book. Turner's reading of the wider travel literature and of the European history of his time must also have enhanced his appreciation of Byron.

GIOVANNI BATTISTA LUSIERI (?1785–?)

21 **The Monument of Philopappos**
Watercolour
902 × 699 (31½ × 23½)
The Earl of Elgin and Kincardine K.T.

The tomb of Philopappos, a Syrian prince and Roman official, was erected by the Athenians between 114 and 116 AD. It stands at the top of the Mouserion Hill.

Lusieri was employed as Elgin's draughtsman in Greece – occupying the post that had been offered to Turner in 1799. He made a series of drawings of architecture and antiquities for his patron, which Turner hoped to see in 1806 (see no.23), but most of them were lost when the ship carrying them to England sank in the Mediterranean. Byron came to know Lusieri in 1809 and 1810; the artist had remained in Athens to oversee the packing and shipment of Elgin's marbles to England, and was able to act as *cicerone* to Byron and Hobhouse; he was moreover the brother-in-law of Nicolo Giraud, Byron's particular friend (and perhaps lover) in Athens. He pointed out the gaps left in the Parthenon and Erectheum sculpture by his patron's removals – to which Byron was already sensitive due to the influence of his cultivated Greek acquaintances – and earned himself a footnote in *Childe Harold* I as 'the agent of devastation … the able instrument of plunder'. However, Byron admitted that 'his works, as far as they go, are most beautiful', adding that they 'are almost all unfinished'. Lusieri was still in Athens when Turner's friend Charles Eastlake visited the city in May 1818, and proved an agreeable guide.

GIOVANNI BATTISTA LUSIERI (?1785–?)

22 Study of an Owl
Watercolour
Oval, 255 × 305 (10 × 12)
The Earl of Elgin and Kincardine K.T.

This owl roosted in the pediment of the Parthenon, and in addition to this charming sketch, Lusieri apparently painted it in one of his architectural subjects in lieu of the emblem usually depicted in Athena's hand.

23 Fight of Centaurs and Lapithae *c.*1804
Pen and ink, pencil and chalk
464 × 624 (18¼ × 24⁹/₁₆)
TB CXX W
D08237

The battle of the Centaurs and the Lapiths is recounted by Homer in the *Iliad* and *Odyssey*, and by Ovid in *Metamorphoses*. It is depicted on the pediment of the Temple of Zeus at Olympia and in the Elgin marbles from the Parthenon at Athens, which arrived in England in 1804. This drawing, perhaps a composition study for a projected painting, was almost certainly made before the marbles were unpacked, and the complex, circular arrangement of the figures owes nothing to the horizontality of the Parthenon frieze. Rather the drawing reflects Turner's reading of classical literature and interest in Greek mythology and history that made him so receptive to the marbles when they were displayed in London in 1807. Having presumably been given a preview of the marbles in 1806, Turner wrote to Elgin to 'pay my homage to your lordships exertions for this rescue from barbarism', and to express his wish to see the drawings made for Elgin by his draughtsman in Athens, Lusieri (see nos.21, 22). In 1799 Turner had himself been offered the post of draughtsman to Elgin, so retained a special interest in his collection.

Byron's attitude to Elgin was the opposite of Turner's. In *Childe Harold* 1 Byron censured him as a sacrilegious thief, asking bitterly

> But who, of all the plunderers of yon fane
> On high, where Pallas linger'd, loth to flee
> The latest relic of her ancient reign;
> The last, the worst dull spoiler, who was he?
> Blush, Caledonia! such thy son could be!

24 **Classical Composition** *c*.1805
Pen and ink, with touches of watercolour
328 × 479 (12⁷/₈ × 18⁷/₈)
Inscribed: 'Homer Reciting to the Greeks his Hymn
to Apollo' and 'Atalus declaring the Greek State to
be Free'
TB CXX Z verso
D04000

A rudimentary sketch for a classical composition whose
alternative subjects from antiquity incorporate the ideas
of national pride and independent identity. The ironic
contrast with modern Greece, enslaved by the Turks, is
implicit in Turner's design, and anticipates Byron's very
pointed contrasts in *Childe Harold*.

25 **The Temple of Aphaia at Aegina** *c*.1814
Pen and ink and brown wash
195 × 292 (7³/₄ × 11³/₈)
TB CXVIII S
D08173

Known to Turner and his contemporaries as the Temple
of Jupiter Panhellenius, this great Doric temple at Aegina
is now recognised as dedicated to the mother-goddess
Aphaia. It was the subject of extensive excavations by an
Anglo-German team in 1811 (see also no.27); the Aegina
marbles are now in the Glyptothek at Munich. Turner
subsequently came to know C.R. Cockerell, the chief
British excavator of the temple, and other architects who
had been in Greece or discussed the excavations with him,
Thomas Allason and T.L. Donaldson. Earlier, he came
into contact with the author and antiquary Henry Gally
Knight, who had travelled in Greece in 1810–11; an old
schoolfriend and fellow student of Byron, Knight had renewed his acquaintance in Athens. He had also visited
Aegina and made a drawing of it which he passed on to
Turner, who probably used it as the foundation of this un-
used design for his series of characteristic landscape types,
the *Liber Studiorum*. A similar view of the ruins in a lush
pastoral landscape appeared in one of the two large paintings of the temple that Turner exhibited in 1816, 'View
of the Temple of Jupiter Panellenius ... with the Greek
National Dance of the Romaika ... Painted from a Sketch
Taken by Henry Gally Knight, Esq. in 1810', (the Duke of
Northumberland; B&J 134). The companion picture
showed the temple elaborately restored (cat.no.26). On
both paintings and their iconography, see J. Gage, 'Turner
and the Greek Spirit', *Turner Studies*, vol.1, no.2, 1981,
pp.14–25.

JOHN PYE (1782–1874) AFTER J.M.W. TURNER

26 **The Temple of Jupiter Panhellenius in the Island of Aegina** 1827
Line engraving, proof of published state (R208d)
383 × 580 (15¹/₁₆ × 22¹³/₁₆) on india paper laid on
wove paper 584 × 805 (23 × 31¹¹/₁₆); plate-mark
522 × 675 (20⁹/₁₆ × 26⁹/₁₆)
Engraved inscriptions below image: 'J.M.W. Turner
R.A.' bottom left, 'John Pye London 1827'
bottom right
T05080

One of a pair of paintings of the Aegina temple shown at the Royal Academy in 1816, 'The Temple of Jupiter Panellenius Restored' (Private Collection, New York; fig.4 on p.22) was based on the drawing provided by Henry Gally Knight, and perhaps on architectural and archaeological evidence gleaned from Thomas Allason, who had been in contact with Cockerell in Athens in 1814.

The two paintings of the temple, ruined and restored, were Turner's first pair contrasting ancient and modern life. The restored temple is seen beyond a landscape with a wedding procession, and at left there is a sculpted relief depicting the victorious chariot of the sun. The themes of dawn and generation implied by these motifs were further developed by Turner's quotation in the Academy catalogue from Southey's poem *Roderick, the Last of the Goths*, describing the trees of the forest, lit by the morning sun, arising 'like pillars of the temple'. The theme of the painting is, essentially, the birth of a civilisation. Its companion piece shows the temple in ruins at sunset, while in the foreground girls dance the Romaika, a national dance surviving from ancient times. This motif of the dance was evidently inspired by Gally Knight's poem *Phrosyne: A Grecian Tale* (1813; published in 1817), which in turn was influenced by Byron's lament for the loss of Greek liberty in *Childe Harold*. Turner's two pictures of the temple show him completely attuned to Byron's political attitudes in the context of Greece, and sharing the poet's method of poignant or ironic contrast between past and present.

27 **The Temple of Aphaia at Aegina, during Excavations*** *c.*1825
Watercolour
267 × 432 (11⁵/₈ × 17⁵/₁₆)
Private Collection
W 493

The leading British member of the Anglo-German team excavating at Aegina in 1811 was the young architect C.R. Cockerell. Having first published an article on the Aegina marbles in the *Journal of Arts and Sciences* in 1819, by 1821 Cockerell was planning a substantial publication on the temple, and had approached Turner to illustrate it. This watercolour is apparently the only survivor of a project for which Turner seems to have done very little as late as 1825: Cockerell's book, *The Temples of Jupiter Panellenius at Aegina and of Apollo Epicurus at Bassae*, with a plate after this design, did not appear until 1860. According to Thornbury (*Life and Correspondence of Turner*, 1877, p.179), Turner charged Cockerell 35 guineas for this subject, which the architect thought exhorbitant. Based on drawings provided by Cockerell – though Turner had already seen drawings made at the temple by Gally Knight, and had drawn and painted it himself (see nos.25, 26) – this watercolour is one of the most impressive and convincing reconstructions of one of the great temples of Greece as Byron must have seen them.

Turner's copy of the Revd Thomas S. Hughes's *Travels in Sicily, Greece and Albania*, 1820, contained an account of the Aegina excavations (see no.29).

**28 The Temple of Poseidon at Sunium
(Cape Colonna)*** *c.*1834
Watercolour, pencil and scraping-out
375 × 584 (14³/₄ × 23)
Private Collection
W 497

This magnificent watercolour, which has not apparently been shown since the exhibition of Old Masters at the Royal Academy in 1877, returns on a grander scale to the subject Turner had meanwhile illustrated for Finden's *Landscape Illustrations* to Byron (no.52). As he had for the Byron illustration, he doubtless used Thomas Allason's drawing, but the viewpoint and mood are here transformed. The sharpness of the promontory and the grandeur of the Doric arcades are given greater emphasis, while the gloriously stormy sky with its baleful sun and flash of lightning, and an almost audible wind, lend sublimity to the remoteness of the scene. The cape was famous for storms, shipwrecks and piracy, and as Byron had reminded his readers, was the actual site of the poet Falconer's shipwreck, from which only he and two others escaped. Turner had long been familiar with the poem, *The Shipwreck*, and, in William Brockedon's notes to Finden's *Landscape Illustrations* I, appeared Falconer's lines:

> And o'er the surge Colonna frowns on high,
> Where marble columns, long by time defaced,
> Moss-covered, on the lofty cape are placed
>
> …
>
> The circling beach in murderous form appears,
> Decisive goal of all their hopes and fears;
> The seamen now in wild amazement see
> The scene of ruin rise beneath their lee.

A ship in trouble may be seen off the shore on the left of the promontory, and Turner's watercolour as a whole realises very fully Brockedon's description: 'Nor is Cape Colonna less destructive in tempestuous weather, when, with awful contrast, this strikingly beautiful scene from the promontory, to which every traveller who has witnessed it bears testimony, exhibits its terrors under the effects of the storms which sometimes frightfully rage around its scathed head'. Brockedon also quoted Dodwell's *Tour through Greece*, on the 'dark green shrubs', the 'metopae scattered among the ruins', and the fallen columns 'below the temple, to which they form the richest foreground'; all these elements are combined here. It was perhaps also Eastlake's recollection of painting 'the darkest blue sea that I suppose ever was painted', during a visit to Sunium in 1818, that prompted Turner's rich colouring.

The purpose of Turner's watercolour is unknown, though its mingled inspiration, beginning with Byron, may be readily reconstructed. However, the fact that it was engraved in 1854 by J.T. Willmore (R 673) permits at least a hypothesis. Willmore had been engraving Turner's work since 1828, but his first large plate was engraved in 1834 from Eastlake's 'Lord Byron's "Dream"' (no.19). In view of the associations Byron and Eastlake shared with Sunium, a view of it could hardly have been a better companion for that print; and this composition would match it perfectly. We know that Turner commissioned Willmore to engrave a large plate for him in the early 1830s but it was delayed owing to the engraver's family priorities (see Gage, *Correspondence*, p.299), and instead a firm arrangement was made for Willmore to engrave another subject, *Mercury and Argus* (R 650). The watercolour of Sunium may well have been the subject originally proposed.

29 Travels in Sicily, Greece and Albania
Thomas Smart Hughes, *Travels in Sicily, Greece and Albania by the Rev. Thos Smart Hughes Late Fellow of St Johns and now Fellow of Emanuel College Cambridge. Illustrated with Engravings, Scenery … in two volumes.*
London, printed for J. Mawman, 39 Ludgate Street, 1820
each 287 × 234 (11¹/₄ × 9¹/₄)
Vol.1 open at pp.282–3: 'Mr Cockerell's Discoveries at Aegina'
Private Collection
[Not illustrated]

Turner's own copy, acquired perhaps on the advice of Cockerell himself, by whom Turner was now engaged to make drawings of Aegina to illustrate a publication by the architect on his excavations at the temple (see nos.25, 27). This account of a visit to Aegina includes mention of Byron, encountered at Piraeus at the outset of the voyage.

30 History of Modern Europe

Walter Fawkes, *The Chronology of the History of Modern Europe from the Extinction of the Western Empire A.D.1475 to the Death of Louis the Sixteenth … In Ten Epochs by Walter Fawkes Esquire*
York, 1810
320 × 261 (12³/₄ × 10¹/₄)
Private Collection
[Not illustrated]

The title-page bears lines from Young's *Night Thoughts*, IX:

When down thy vale, unlock'd by Midnight-Thought,
That loves to wander in thy sunless realms,
O Death! I sketch my view, what visions rise!
What triumphs, toils imperial! arts divine!
In wither'd laurels glide before my sight!
What lengths of far-fam'd ages, billow'd high
With human agitation, roll along
In unsubstantial images of air!
The melancholy ghosts of dead renown
Whispering faint echoes of the world's applause,
With penitential aspect, as they pass,
All point at earth, and hiss at human pride,
The wisdom of the wise, and prancings of the great.

Exhibited in the presentation copy he gave to Turner, with the 'author's kindest regards', Fawkes's book is essentially a concordance of dates and genealogies, a convenient historical primer. Nevertheless his choice of introductory quotation proclaims the romantic, emotive view of history that he shared with Turner and Byron. Young's declaration, 'I sketch my view, what visions rise!' must have summed up the panoramic landscapes and human narratives that lay behind Fawkes's bald lists, just as it could also speak for the rich associations Turner assumed would be recognised in his own views of continental Europe. Byron's skill in elucidating these in *Childe Harold*, two years after Fawkes's book was published, was certainly the basis of his appeal to Fawkes and Turner, and it was probably Fawkes who helped to bring Byron to Turner's attention. If Fawkes was also attracted to the melancholy and ironic tone of Young's lines, he would have found Byron's exposition of the lessons of history powerfully appealing.

31 A Journey to Rome and Naples

Henry Sass, *A Journey to Rome and Naples Performed in 1817 Giving an Account of the Present State of Society in Italy and Containing Observations on the Fine Arts by Henry Sass, Student of the Royal Academy of Arts*
London, printed for Longman, Hurst, Rees, Orme and Brown, Paternoster Row 1818
232 × 150 (9¹/₈ × 5⁷/₈)
Private Collection
[Not illustrated]

Turner's own copy of a book by one of his friends. Sass's guide was one of those he consulted for his first tour of Italy in 1819, and it summed up the Romantic apprehension of its manifold historical associations, as Byron did poetically in *Childe Harold*: 'what throbs filled my breast, when about to visit the country of the Horatii and Curatii, of Junius Brutus, of Mutius, of Cincinnatus, of Camillus, … of Caesar, Cicero, and Seneca … of Virgil, Horace, Ovid, and Quintilian, of the Antonines! What delight to range over the hills of Rome – the Palatine where Romulus was found – the Aventine where the Romans so often made a stand for liberty – the Capitoline where sat an assemblage of gods, as the Roman Senate has been described.'

32 A Picturesque Tour

J. Mawman, *A Picturesque Tour through France, Switzerland, on the Banks of the Rhine, and through Part of the Netherlands in the Year* MDCCCXVI
London, printed for J. Mawman, 39 Ludgate Street, 1817
232 × 153 (9¹/₈ × 6)
Private Collection
[Not illustrated]

Turner's own copy. Freshly published, this, together with Charles Campbell's *Traveller's Complete Guide through Belgium and Holland … with a Sketch of a Tour in Germany* (2nd ed., 1817), was acquired just in time for Turner's journey to Waterloo and the Rhineland in 1817. He had also prepared himself by taking notes from two larger illustrated volumes by the print-seller Robert Hills, and the Revd John Gardnor (see C. Powell, *Turner's Rivers of Europe: The Rhine, Meuse and Mosel*, Tate Gallery, London 1991, p.21).

JOHN LANDSEER (1769–1852) AFTER
J.M.W. TURNER

33 **Cascade of Terni** 1819
Line-engraving, published state (R 145)
218 × 142 (8⁹/₁₆ × 5⁹/₁₆) on plain paper 252 × 150
(9¹⁵/₁₆ × 5¹⁵/₁₆); cut within plate-mark
Engraved inscriptions: '*Drawn by J.M.W. Turner R.A.
from a finish'd sketch by James Hakewill*', below image
bottom left, '*Engrav'd by John Landseer F.S.A.*' below
image bottom right, '*Cascade of Terni*' below image
at centre
T06013

In 1818, at the very time when *Childe Harold* IV was published, Turner was occupied in making watercolours to
illustrate James Hakewill's *Picturesque Tour of Italy*. Not having yet been to Italy himself, he depended on the author's
own drawings, and on impressions gleaned from his reading. His view of the waterfalls at Terni precisely matches
the description and mood of Byron's lines in *Childe Harold*
(IV.lixix, lixxii):

> The roar of waters! – from the headlong height
> Velino cleaves the wave-worn precipice;
> The fall of waters! rapid as the light
> The flashing mass foams shaking the abyss …

Fittingly, this passage from 'a great modern poet' was
quoted by Hakewill in his text, providing the first published conjunction of Byron's poetry and Turner's art.

JOHN BYRNE (1786–1847) AFTER J.M.W. TURNER

34 **Tomb of Cecilia Metella** 1819
Line-engraving, published state (R153)
139 × 216 (5¹/₂ × 8¹/₂) on plain paper 168 × 224
(6⁷/₈ × 8¹³/₁₆); cut within plate-mark
Engraved inscriptions: '*Drawn by J.M.W. Turner R.A.
from a finish'd sketch by James Hakewill*' below image
bottom left. '*Engraved by John Byrne*' below image
bottom right, 'Tomb of Cecilia Metella' below image
at centre
T06021

Another design for Hakewill's *Italy*, anticipating Turner's
later rendering of the subject for Finden's *Landscape Illustrations* (no.56).

TURNER'S BYRONIC PAINTINGS

Between 1818 and 1844, Turner exhibited six paintings with quotations from Byron. Together these pictures, like Byron's poetry itself, provide a remarkable survey of modern Europe from North to South, from the battlefield of Waterloo to the post-Napoleonic era.

35 The Field of Waterloo* RA 1818
Oil on canvas
1475 × 2390 (58 × 94)
Turner Bequest
B&J 138
N00500

This dark and terrible picture of women searching for their loved ones among the mingled dead – French *cuirassiers* and Scottish infantrymen – by the baleful light of flares and the burning farm of Hougoumont, was exhibited with lines adapted from *Childe Harold* III.xxviii:

'Last noon behold them full of lusty life;
Last even in Beauty's circle proudly gay;
The midnight brought the signal-sound of strife;
The morn the marshalling of arms – the day,
Battle's magnificently stern array!
The thunder clouds close o'er it, which when rent,
The earth is covered thick with other clay
Which her own clay shall cover, heaped and pent,
Rider and horse – friend, foe, in one red burial blent!'

This was Turner's first painting to be shown with a text from Byron, and one of the earliest to be amplified thus in the Royal Academy catalogue. If he had not already read Byron's poem in fuller form, he would have found these lines on Waterloo reprinted in the guidebook he had taken with him when visiting the battlefield in August 1817 – a revised edition published earlier that year of Charles

Campbell's *Traveller's Complete Guide to Belgium and Holland*. The *Times* had also reprinted them shortly after their first appearance. Turner adopted Byron's grimly realistic vision of the aftermath of battle as his own, producing the absolute opposite of the conventional battle picture, avoiding overt celebration of victory and stressing instead the more universal moral of the remorseless wheel of fortune, which had not only brought a tyrant to his inevitable destruction but had carried so many British officers straight from the Duchess of Richmond's ball in Brussels to their last battle.

Like Byron, who in 1816 had ridden over the battlefield on a Cossack horse and paused 'in a musing mood', to gather a number of melancholy souvenirs, Turner was able to base his interpretation on personal research. On 16 August 1817 he filled seventeen pages of his sketchbooks with memoranda of the field and notes of the progress of the battle, gleaned not only from his reading but from the guide who escorted him – one of a number who swiftly emerged to serve a generation of travellers well aware of the epic nature of an event which had literally decided the future course of their century. Byron thought the site compared badly to other great battlefields of history – 'a fine one, but not much after Marathon and Troy', he told Hobhouse – and admitted his true feelings about Waterloo to the same friend. For him it was impossible to celebrate a victory that had restored reactionary tyranny or its dynastic dependents across much of continental Europe; 'I detest the cause and the victors – and the victory – including Blucher and the Bourbons'. Such sentiments clearly underlie his account in *Childe Harold*, as friends like Walter Scott well understood, and Turner's bleak realisation of carnage, inviting human compassion and grief rather than national rejoicing, could well have exposed him to criticism. His purpose, however, was surely not political, but to tell what seemed to him to be the truth, as nearly as he could reconstruct it, and to condemn the folly and futility of ambition and empire-building.

Fittingly, he returned to this conception when preparing his Waterloo vignette for the *Life and Works* of Byron (see no.75) and a very similar rendering of the dead on the battlefield was among the watercolours based on his 1817 visit acquired that year by Walter Fawkes (Fitzwilliam Museum, Cambridge). For a preparatory study probably connected with Fawkes's watercolour, or with a proposed vignette based on it, see no.76.

36 Childe Harold's Pilgrimage – Italy* RA 1832

Oil on canvas
1420 × 2480 (56 × 97³/₄)
Turner Bequest
B&J 342
N00516

Exhibited with lines taken from *Childe Harold* IV.iv:

' – and now, fair Italy!
Thou art the garden of the world.
Even in they desert what is like to thee?
Thy very weeds are beautiful, thy waste
More rich than other climes' fertility:
Thy wreck a glory, and thy ruin graced
With an immaculate charm which cannot be defaced'
                    Lord Byron, Canto 4

Formed alike on the paintings of Claude – by which Turner's own impressions of Italy and those of generations of his compatriots had been nurtured – and on an assemblage of his own observations during his visits in 1819 and 1828, this painting presents a definitive statement of the enduring beauty of Italy. Byron's concept of a country decayed and diminished, spread with the ruins of its glorious past, yet redeemed by the beauties of nature, was one to which Turner was deeply receptive, and he has given it magnificent exposition in this warm and tender landscape. Although Ruskin observed that the scenery on the right is 'founded on faithful reminiscences of the Defiles of Narni, and the roots of the Apennines', and there are other factual elements, the view as a whole is imaginary, and may have been composed to evoke the setting of the following stanzas of *Childe Harold,* in which Byron alluded to Petrarch, who 'arose/to raise a language, and his land reclaim/From the dull yoke of her barbaric foes', and whose mountain village of Arqua had itself become a place of pilgrimage. Thus, as often in *Childe Harold* when writing of Italy or Greece, Byron had sought to sow seeds of national revival through an emotive appeal to the past, while acknowledging the imperfections of the present – for meanwhile the charms of Arqua provide 'a refuge from … hopes decay'd'. It would have been fitting indeed if

Turner had taken Byron's tribute to a former poet as the setting for his own tribute to Byron, through this realisation of the sad and beautiful land they both loved.

The Bright Stone of Honour (Ehrenbreitstein), and Tomb of Marceau, from Byron's 'Childe Harold'* RA 1835

Oil on canvas
930 × 1230 (36⁵/₈ × 48⁷/₁₆)
Private Collection
B&J 361
[Not exhibited]

This sparkling painting was made for the engraver John Pye, who in 1828 had engraved one of Turner's earlier views of Ehrenbreitstein (no.87) for *The Literary Souvenir* (R 317a). It was finally reproduced, after considerable impatience on Turner's part, in a beautiful large plate in 1846 (R 662). Pye had apparently first expected a watercolour, but Turner produced a splendid example of his mature handling of oil, distinguished by a rich, warm palette and diaphanous effects of brilliant light. The subject is the great castle of Ehrenbreitstein (or 'broad stone of honour') above Coblenz, with the stone pyramid erected to the memory of the French soldier Marceau. Turner had visited Ehrenbreitstein during his Rhine tour in 1817, and Byron had described his earlier impressions of the place to Hobhouse:

at Coblentz crossed the Rhine – and scrambled up the fortress of Ehrenbreitstein now a ruin – we also saw on the road the sepulchres – & monuments of Generals Marceau & Hoche & went up to examine them – they are simple & striking – but now much neglected if not to say defaced by the change of times.

For the painting, Turner adapted the lines Byron contributed to *Childe Harold* III.lvi–lviii:

> By Coblentz, on a rise of gentle ground,
> There is a small and simple pyramid,
> Crowning the summit of the verdant mound;
> Beneath its base are heroes' ashes hid,
> Our enemy's – but let that not forbid
> Honour to Marceau ——
> —— He was freedom's champion!
> Here Ehrenbreitstein, with her shattered wall,
> Yet shows of what she was.

Like the Maid of Saragossa (see no.11), Marceau was one of those modern heroes and exemplars whom Byron assimilated into the landscape of his poem, expressing thereby his impartiality and wider European sympathies. General Marceau had made his reputation during the Revolution and in the campaigns that followed, being promoted general at the age of only twenty-four. After participating in unsuccessful French attacks on the fortress of Ehrenbreitstein in 1795 and 1796, he was given command of the first division of the Sambre-et-Meuse army. While covering their retreat at the Battle of Altenkirchen in September 1796, he was killed by the bullet of an Austrian huntsman. His body was escorted back to Neuwied by the Rhine by 2,000 soldiers led by their generals, and buried with full honours near the headquarter of the Sambre-et-Meuse army north of Coblenz. By the wishes of the Austrian commander Archduke Charles, the Austrian army joined the French in paying their respects, attending the funeral and firing a volley over the grave. The stone pyramid (today in a different spot) was erected on his tomb. Turner's painting shows the armies by their tents in the distance near the tomb; an Austrian soldier in his white and scarlet uniform is prominent in the group of figures by the fountain. The fortress appears in ruins, as Turner and Byron remembered it, following its demolition prior to reconstruction after the war.

37 **Modern Rome – Campo Vaccino*** RA 1839
Oil on canvas
902 × 1220 (35½ × 48)
B&J 379
The Earl of Rosebery, on loan to the National Gallery of Scotland

Exhibited with lines adapted from *Childe Harold* IV.xxvii:

> 'The moon is up and yet it is not night,
> The sun as yet divides the day with her'.

In Byron's original the second line reads:

> Sunset divides the sky with her – a sea.

'Modern Rome' was painted as a companion to 'Ancient Rome; Agrippina Landing with the Ashes of Germanicus. the Triumphal Bridge and Palace of the Caesars Restored' (Tate Gallery; B&J 378). The contrast between ancient and modern civilisations was one that Turner frequently addressed in pairs of pictures, and these canvases shown in 1839 developed in a specifically Roman context themes he had presented in an earlier pair, 'Ancient Italy' and 'Modern Italy' shown in 1838 (B&J 375, 374). In the 1839 pair, the historical episode represented in 'Ancient Rome' is to be seen as a stage in the moral decline of Rome, which in 'Modern Rome' has become manifest through the physical decay of the Forum. As the *Art Union* declared of this picture; 'The glory has departed. The eternal city, with its splendours – its stupendous temples, and its great men – all have become a mockery and a scorn. The plough has gone over its grandeurs, and weeds have grown in its high places'. Such observations had been made by a host of eighteenth-century travellers and writers, but among Turner's contemporaries Byron had given them their clearest, and most deeply ironic literary expression. Turner however did not choose his quotation from one of the specifically Roman passages of *Childe Harold*. His intention was to allow the city to speak for itself through the poignant contrast of structural decay and natural beauty, and the correlation implied in the lines he did choose between the processes inevitably affecting man-made things and the eternal cycle of time and seasons. Rome, beautiful even when crumbling and overgrown, is shown suspended between a magnificent past and an uncertain future as between day and night.

38 **Venice, the Bridge of Sighs*** RA 1840
Oil on canvas
610 × 915 (24 × 36)
Turner Bequest
B&J 383
N00527

Exhibited with lines reduced from *Childe Harold* IV.i:

'I stood upon a bridge, a palace and
A prison on each hand' – *Byron*

Byron's lines, opening the final canto, actually read:

I stood in Venice, on the Bridge of Sighs;
A palace and a prison on each hand.

The contrast of palace and prison is of course precisely that to be found in Venice, where the Doge's Palace is connected to the prison by the Bridge of Sighs, but as Byron, and Turner after him, fully realised, the splendours of the city's past had been matched by grimmer realities of incarceration and torture. The prospect of modern Venice, moreover, offered a further irony – the once splendid city, full of the palazzi of its old nobility and merchants, had itself become a prison for its people,

Where now the Austrian reigns –
An Emperor tramples where an Emperor knelt;
Kingdoms are shrunk to provinces, and chains
Clank over sceptred cities; nations melt
From power's high pinnacle, when they have felt
The sunshine for a while, and downward go.

If we may judge from Turner's title for a Venetian picture of 1833, 'The Sun of Venice Going to Sea' (Tate Gallery; B&J 402) – based perhaps on these very lines – Turner was as thoroughly susceptible to Byron's image of Venice as a paradigm for the downward curve of history as he was to his decisive picture of the mingled luxury and cruelty of its magnificent past.

ROBERT WALLIS (1794–1878) AFTER
J.M.W. TURNER

39 **The Approach to Venice** 1859
Line engraving, engraver's proof (R 679 b)
397 × 595 (15⅝ × 23⁷⁄₁₆) on india paper laid on wove paper 644 × 822 (25⅜ × 32⅜); plate-mark 583 × 731 (22¹⁵⁄₁₆ × 28¾)
T05193

Turner's painting 'Approach to Venice'* (National Gallery of Art, Washington D.C.; B&J 412) was exhibited at the Royal Academy in 1844, with two quotations, firstly from Rogers's *Italy*:

'The path lies o'er the sea invisible,
And from the land we went
As to a floating city, steering in,
And gliding up her streets as in a dream,
So smoothly, silently.'

and secondly (in modified form) from *Childe Harold* IV.xxvii:

'The moon is up, and yet it is not night,
The sun as yet disputes the day with her.'

Turner had changed Byron's verb 'divides' to 'disputes'. The Rogers quotation is in fact the more appropriate to the picture, Byron's lines seeming perhaps something of an afterthought. However, this was one of Turner's favourite and most meaningful passages in Byron, matching his own oft-repeated image of the approaching night as both beautiful and ominous, and as a symbol of decay. For him as for Byron, Venice was as much a city of the night as of day, and here, as gondolas gather in the lagoon, a world of possibilities, good and bad, is evoked.

Wallis's print was published as a single plate, posthumously in 1859.

GEORGE HOLLIS (1793–1842) AFTER
J.M.W. TURNER

40 **St Mark's Place, Venice: Juliet and her Nurse**
1842
Line-engraving, first published state (R 654)
423 × 564 (16⅝ × 22⁵⁄₁₆) on wove paper 660 × 772
(26 × 30⅜); plate-mark 539 × 652 (21¼ × 25¹¹⁄₁₆)
Engraved inscriptions: 'Painted by JMW Turner RA.'
below image bottom left, 'Engrav^d. by G. Hollis.'
below image bottom right, 'LONDON: PUBLISHED
JUNE 23rd 1842, BY THO^s. GRIFFITH, ESQ.^re 14
WATERLOO PLACE, FOR J.M.W. TURNER, R.A.'
below image at centre
T05188

Turner's highly important and controversial painting
'Juliet and her Nurse' (Private Collection; B&J 365) was
exhibited at the Royal Academy in 1836. The cruel attack
made upon it by the Revd John Eagles in *Blackwood's Magazine* that year moved the young John Ruskin to write a
letter in Turner's defence – which the artist advised him
not to publish. The anachronistic transposition of a passionate moment from *Romeo and Juliet* (Act II, scene ii) to
Venice – though presumably justified in Turner's eyes by
the palpably romantic atmosphere of Venice by night –
was among the more understandable of Eagles's com-
plaints and it may have been partly to concede the point
that Turner substantially changed the emphasis of the second state of this print, connecting it instead with Byron's
vision of a city of universal entertainment and romantic
desire. The second state bore the new title, 'St Mark's
Place, Venice (Moonlight)', and a quotation reduced from
Childe Harold IV:

> but Beauty doth not die –
> Nor yet forget how Venice once was dear –
> The pleasant place of all festivity
> The revels of the earth, the Masque of Italy

PUBLISHED ILLUSTRATIONS

Turner's very finest illustration to Byron in watercolour
was a private commission from his friend Walter Fawkes,
and was never engraved or published. His illustrations to
Byron's life and poetry made for publication fall into two
groups. Listed first are nine landscape subjects, made for
William Finden and John Murray. These were originally
intended to illustrate *Childe Harold* in particular and
Byron's relevant travels in general, with an accompanying
memoir or travelogue by J.C. Hobhouse. For a fuller account of the project and its failure, see Introduction.
When the text by Hobhouse failed to materialise, it was
decided to publish the landscape plates together with
those meanwhile commissioned by Murray to illustrate a
popular monthly parts edition of Moore's *Life and Works of
Byron*; the result was Finden's *Landscape Illustrations to
Mr. Murray's First Complete and Uniform Edition of The Life and
Works of Lord Byron*. Turner's seventeen vignette subjects, issued with the landscapes in *Landscape Illustrations* but made
expressly for the frontispieces and title pages of *Life and
Works*, and first published there, are also listed below. See
Introduction for this project besides. Examples of all the
plates after Turner are included here, either in the paper
parts of Finden or in the bound *Life and Works* volumes;
one example is included of the landscape plates reissued
in 1833 with a text by William Brockedon; and where possible Turner's original watercolours are also shown.

Illustration to 'The Giaour': The Acropolis, Athens* 1822
Watercolour and pencil
187 × 127 (7⁷/₁₆ × 5⁵/₁₆)
Inscribed 'J M W Turner RA 1822' below left of image, 'T''is living Greece no more' at lower centre
Vouros-Eutaxias Museum of the City of Athens
W 1055
[Not exhibited]

This was Turner's first illustration to Byron in watercolour, and remains his most penetrating exposition of a specific Byronic text. It was made, with other illustrations to Scott and Moore, for Walter Fawkes; with a frontispiece showing the three poets, it was presumably intended – like Turner's other watercolours documenting the Farnley estates, the family history or its ornithological interests – to illustrate volumes in the Farnley library. Fawkes was evidently fond of Byron's poetry, and as a patrician radical concerned for principles of freedom at home and abroad, and interested in the history and contemporary condition of Europe, he must have found much of substance as well as of style to admire in it. In illustrating a climactic line from the opening passage of *The Giaour*, Turner has created a profound and moving work. Rising above the merely picturesque exoticism, sentimentality and gruesomeness of many illustrators of the Oriental tales (see for examples George Jones's drawings from this poem, nos.13, 14), he focused instead on Byron's more significant message – the miseries of a subject people, ironically enacted within the shadow of their own magnificent past. This was Turner's first depiction of modern Athens, assembled from records by others who had travelled there. The Acropolis rises above the plain, and slumped in the foreground are two manacled Greek girls, slaves whose Turkish guardian lounges beside them. Behind, as a backdrop to this sad tableau, is a fragment from the Parthenon frieze, probably based on the South metope, no.xxvIII of the Elgin marbles now in London – one of those depicting the battle of the Centaurs and Lapiths that Turner admired above all others (see no.23), and of which he had acquired casts.

Turner never achieved greater insights into the Byronic temper than in this watercolour, although a decade later he returned to a similar viewpoint, and to the motif of the galloping horsemen in the plain, for his view of the Acropolis for Finden's *Landscape Illustrations* to Byron (no.47).

WILLIAM FINDEN (1787–1852)

41 **Lord Byron at the Age of 19**
Line-engraving on india paper 238 × 189
(9¹³/₁₆ × 7¹³/₁₆) laid on wove paper 402 × 334
(15⁶/₈ × 13¹/₈); plate-mark 404 × 340 (15³/₄ × 13¹/₂)
Engraved inscriptions: 'Painted by G. Sanders' below image bottom left, 'Engraved by W. Finden' below image bottom right, 'Lord Byron/at the age of 19/ Engraved from the original Picture in the possession of John Cam Hobhouse Esqʳᵉ M.P. to whom this plate is respectfully dedicated. London. Published Novʳ 6 1830 by Moon, Boys & Graves, Pall Mall, for the Proprietor, John Murray, Albemarle Street' below image at centre
Private Collection

Finden engraved this plate after Sanders's portrait (no.1) as the frontispiece to the first edition of Murray's edition of Moore's *Life* of Byron. The lettering, together with that added to his brother Edward's plate engraved from the portrait in 1834, establishes that Sanders painted it in 1807. Hobhouse asked for some modifications to be made to the plate before publication, and it was while at work on these that Finden proposed his plan of illustrating Byron 'topographically', and secured, as he supposed, Hobhouse's agreement to provide accompanying text (see Introduction).

AFTER HENRY WILLIAM PICKERSGILL (1782–1875)

42 **John Murray**
Mezzotint, oval 145 × 114 (5¹¹/₁₆ × 4⁷/₁₆) on wove
paper 226 × 160 (8⁹/₁₆ × 6¹/₄); plate-mark;
238 × 171 (9⁷/₁₆ × 6⁵/₈)
Engraved inscriptions: 'Yours affectionately/John
Murray/BORN 1778–DIED 1843/From the Portrait
by Pickersgill. R.A.' below image at centre
Private Collection

John Murray (1778–1843), Byron's friend and publisher.
He issued Finden's *Landscape Illustrations* (no.45) and the
edition of Moore's *Life and Works* (no.59) with Turner's
illustrations. This print, by an unknown engraver, is a
reduction from Pickersgill's portrait still in the Murray collection, showing the publisher reading a manuscript, with
a bust of Byron at his side.

WILLIAM HENRY WATT (b.1804) AFTER GILBERT
STUART NEWTON (1795–1835)

43 **Thomas Moore** 1828
Mezzotint 278 × 218 (10⁷/₈ × 8⁶/₈) on wove paper
421 × 315 (17¹/₂ × 12¹/₄); plate-mark 360 × 275
(14¹/₈ × 10¹⁵/₁₆)
Engraved inscriptions: 'Painted by G.S Newton'
below image bottom left, 'Engraved by W.H. Watt'
below image bottom right, 'THOMAS MOORE ESQ^R'
and 'London published June 1828 by W.H. Watt'
below image centre
Private Collection

The Irish poet Thomas Moore (1779–1852) first met Byron
in Samuel Rogers's house in November 1811, and became
his close and loyal friend. He knew Turner by 1819, and
met him in Rome that year shortly after visiting Byron in
Venice. Byron had entrusted Moore with his memoirs on
that occasion, but in 1821 Moore's financial embarass-
ments obliged him to pawn the manuscript to Murray;
later, on Hobhouse's order, it was destroyed. Moore's biography of Byron, published by Murray in 1830, was
inevitably less vivid than it would have been had he had
access to Byron's original material, or indeed been able to
secure the co-operation of Hobhouse; nevertheless it is a
sincere and sensitive work as far as it goes. For the edition
published with Byron's works and Turner's illustrations,
see no.59 (*Life and Works*).
 Moore had sat to the American painter Gilbert Stuart
Newton in 1821–4, for a miniature now at Bowood.

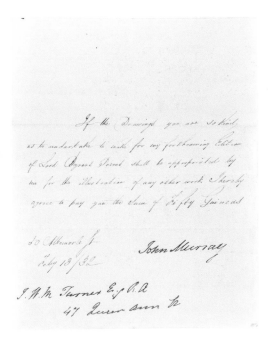

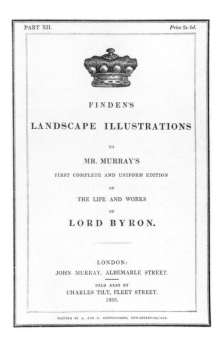

44 Agreement between John Murray and Turner
234 × 192 (9¼ × 7½)
Private Collection

'If the Drawings you are so kind as to undertake for my forthcoming Edition of Lord Byrons Poems shall be appropriated by me for the illustration of any other work I hereby agree to pay you the sum of Fifty Guineas

50 Albemarle Street, John Murray
Feby 13
32
J.M.W. Turner Esq R.A.
47 Queen Ann St'

45 Finden's Landscape Illustrations to Mr. Murray's First Complete and Uniform Edition of the Life and Works of Lord Byron
London, John Murray, 1832–1833
Fifteen parts, each 232 × 169 (9⅛ × 6¾)
Part I open to display prospectus for the
Landscape Illustrations
Part II open to display prospectus for Murray's illustrated edition of *Life and Works* (see no.59)
Private Collection

The prospectus for *Landscape Illustrations* announces fourteen monthly parts to appear from 16 January 1832 (in fact more than twenty were issued), and an allocation per part of four landscapes and one portrait (this also was not strictly adhered to). Each part would cost no more than 2s.6d. Proofs would be taken on plain paper, royal quarto, at 5s., and on india paper, at 7s. 6d. (for example, no.57); with these would appear proofs of the frontispieces and vignettes contained in each volume of the *Life and Works* published concurrently.

The prospectus for *Life and Works* proclaims the publishers' wish to 'place within the reach of all classes of readers these delightful productions of the first Poet of the age'. It announces fourteen monthly volumes, six devoted to Byron's life, correspondence and miscellaneous prose, the remainder to the poetry. Each volume would contain a frontispiece and title vignette 'by eminent artists, from entirely new designs', and would cost 5s. Publication would run from 1 January 1832 to 1 February 1833. Murray states that he has taken copyright on the whole at a 'cost of more than Twenty-Five Thousand Pounds'. Seventeen volumes were published in all (see no.59), edited by John Wright, whose name went unacknowledged.

EDWARD FINDEN (1791–1857) AFTER
J.M.W. TURNER

46 **Gibraltar** *c.*1833
Line-engraving, published state (R 406)
93 × 141 (3¹¹/₁₆ × 5⁹/₁₆) on plain paper
108 × 144 (4¹/₄ × 5¹¹/₁₆); cut within plate-mark
Engraved inscriptions: 'Drawn by J.M.W. Turner,
R.A. from a sketch by G. Reinagle' below image
bottom left, 'Engraved by E. Finden' below image
bottom right, 'GIBRALTAR' below image at centre
T06175

Turner's watercolour (W 1210) is with Messrs Spink. With
that of Malta (see no.50) it was one of the first to be made
in connection with Finden's projected *Landscape Illustrations;* Finden's letter to Hobhouse of 6 October 1830 (see
also Introduction) announced that Turner had undertaken
to submit his drawings of Malta and Gibraltar 'immediately upon his return to Town'. Murray's accounts cite a
payment of £24. 3*s.* for it, probably at some point early
in 1831, and also its subsequent sale, after it had been engraved, for £18. 2*s.* 3*d.* In fact however this subject did
not appear in the first, parts issue of the *Landscape Illustrations,* but was reserved for the 1833 re-issue with
Brockedon's text; published there as the first plate, it must
be the 'new and beautiful frontispiece by Turner' that the
publishers had promised in advance of this revised version
of the *Illustrations.* Brockedon's text quotes three lines from
Childe Harold II.xxii:

> Through Calpe's straits survey the steepy shore;
> Europe and Afric on each other gaze!
> Lands of the dark-eyed Maid and dusky Moor.

Turner's design unites the European and Moorish life of
the straits by including both British vessels and African
feluccas. However, the subject was probably always envis-
aged as a general and introductory one, opening up the
Mediterranean world that is the subject of so much of
Byron's writing, and of all but one of the *Landscape Illustrations.* It alludes besides to Byron's arrival and stay at

Gibraltar in 1809, after travelling down through Portugal
and Spain and before departing for Malta at the start of
his journey to Greece.

Although only the original drawing of Gibralter is accredited to him in the lettering on the plate, it is likely that
both this work and the foundation drawing of Malta were
provided by George Reinagle, who had accompanied
Admiral Codrington's fleet in the Eastern Mediterranean
during the recent campaign for Greek independence.

JOHN COUSEN (1804–1880) AFTER J.M.W. TURNER

47 **The Acropolis, Athens** 1832
Line-engraving, published state (R 408)
94 × 139 (3³/₄ × 5¹/₂) on india paper
106 × 141 (4³/₁₆ × 5⁹/₁₆); cut within plate-mark
Engraved inscriptions: '*Drawn by J.M.W. Turner* from
a Sketch by T. Allison' below image bottom left,
'*Engraved by J. Cousins*' below image bottom right,
'THE ACROPOLIS, ATHENS' below image at centre
T06177

Turner's watercolour (W 1212) is in a private collection.
See nos.48–9 for preparatory colour studies for this subject, evidently showing Turner exploring the formal and
tonal possibilities of the original drawing supplied by
Thomas Allason. Turner's design, with its powerful effect
of sunlight behind the Acropolis, and its vividly dramatic
foreground with Turkish horsemen careering across the
plain raising clouds of dust, in one of the most inspired of
his contributions to Finden's series. The plate was first
published in Finden's *Landscape Illustrations,* part v. Murray's account cite a payment of £21 for the watercolour,
and its sale, after it had been engraved, for fifteen guineas.

Cousen's plate is a masterly realisation of Turner's elaborate conception. A proof formerly in the collection of
W.G. Rawlinson preserves some of Turner's instructions
to the engraver: on the left, 'There are too many small

pieces of paper left white making the work look unsolid';
at centre, foreground, 'This part of the ground too much
of single strokes, line wants strength or crossing'; on the
right, 'These horses are too low in tone'.

49 Two Studies of the Acropolis *c.*1832
Watercolour
377 × 226 (14¹³/₁₆ × 8⁷/₈)
Watermark: W KING 1828
Blind-stamp: BATH SUPERFINE
TB CCLXII 253
D25375, D25376

Two further colour studies, facing in opposite directions
on a folded sheet of paper, showing the progress of
Turner's ideas for his view of the Acropolis for Finden's
Landscape Illustrations to Byron. In the upper half of the
sheet, here seen upside down, the Acropolis and its rock
are more clearly defined in red wash, still seen from the
same angle as in the preceding drawing, no.48. The lower
half of the sheet bears only the faintest indications of the
Acropolis, but the marks of red wash in the foreground
may show Turner evolving the rudiments of the horsemen
that appeared in the finished subject.

48 Athens, the Acropolis *c.*1832
Watercolour
188 × 228 (7³/₈ × 9)
Watermark: 1828
TB CCCLXIV 402
D36270

A colour study, presumably derived with no.49 from the
sketch of the Acropolis by Thomas Allason that Turner
used when preparing his view for Finden's *Landscape Illustrations* to Byron. Presumably both colour studies were
made in connection with the finished design. Here the size
and format is similar to that used for the Finden subject,
and the Acropolis is likewise seen beyond the broad ex-
panse of plain which in the finished version was filled with
columns of galloping horsemen. The angle of vision is
however slightly different.

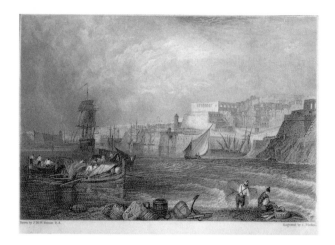

EDWARD FINDEN (1791–1857) AFTER
J.M.W. TURNER

50 **Malta** 1832
Line-engraving, published state (R 407)
94 × 143 (3³/₄ × 5⁵/₈) on paper 108 × 145
(4¹/₄ × 5³/₄), cut within plate-mark
Engraved inscriptions: 'Drawn by J.M.W. Turner
R.A.' below image bottom left, 'Engraved by
E. Finden' below image bottom right, 'MALTA'
below image at centre
T06176

Turner's watercolour (W 1211) has not been located. With
'Gibraltar', it was the first to be made for Finden's *Landscape Illustrations*, and appeared first in part VI, 1832. It was
probably based on a drawing by George Reinagle (see
no.46). Malta and Gozo are 'Calypso's isles', those 'sister
tenants of the middle deep' briefly mentioned in *Childe
Harold* II.xxix, but the subject was more likely to have
been made to introduce an account of Byron's three-week
residence on Malta on his way to Greece in 1809. Turner's
view is of the harbour of Valetta, whose massive forti-
fications emphasise the strategic importance of this British
station in the Mediterranean, while the laden boats in the
foreground proclaim the mercantile prosperity of the island. Murray's accounts cite £24 3s. for the purchase of
the watercolour and drawing, and its subsequent sale after
engraving for fifteen guineas.

51 **Temple of Minerva, Cape Colonna (Sunium)**
1832
Watercolour and bodycolour
160 × 219 (6¹/₂ × 8³/₄)
*Towneley Hall Art Gallery and Museums, Burnley
Borough Council*
W 1213

The subject is the Temple of Poseidon at Sunium, with its
row of white marble Doric columns. Engraved by Edward
Finden for *Landscape Illustrations*, part VIII, this was one of
the subjects specifically related to *Childe Harold* (II.lxxvi):

> Save where Tritonia's airy shrine adorns
> Colonna's cliff, and gleams along the wave.

Murray paid £21 for this watercolour; it was sold after
engraving for fifteen guineas. Byron's notes to the poem
declared, 'In all Attica, if we except Athens itself and
Marathon, there is no scene more interesting than Cape
Colonna', and enumerated its associations with Plato and
the poet Falconer, whose *Shipwreck* recounted a disaster in
these treacherous waters, its interest 'to the antiquary and
artist', and his own encounter with a band of pirates. He
also wrote of Sunium in *The Giaour* and in *Don Juan* III.
Turner's view was based on a drawing by Thomas
Allason. This watercolour is notable for its brilliant effect
of clouded moonlight, whose warm reflection on the
smooth waters of the gulf is contrasted with the predomi-
nantly cold blue tonality. The resting group in the
foreground may have been suggested by two of the suc-
ceeding lines in this stanza from *Childe Harold*:

> While strangers only not regardless pass,
> Lingering like me, perchance, to gaze, and sigh 'Alas!'

For a more dramatic view of Sunium, see no.28.

EDWARD FINDEN (1791–1857) AFTER
J.M.W. TURNER

52 **Temple of Minerva, Cape Colonna** 1832
Line-engraving, published state (R 409)
93 × 136 (3¹¹⁄₁₆ × 5³⁄₈) on plain paper
108 × 139 (4¹⁄₄ × 5¹⁄₂); cut within plate-mark
Engraved inscriptions: 'Drawn by J.M.W. Turner,
R.A. from a sketch by T. Allason, Esq.' below image
bottom left, 'Engraved by E. Finden' below image
bottom right, 'TEMPLE OF MINERVA' below image
at centre
T06178

53 **The Drachenfels** 1833
Watercolour, pencil and scraping-out
128 × 204 (5 × 8)
Manchester City Art Galleries
W 1216

Engraved by William Finden for his *Landscape Illustrations*,
part XI, this was one of the subjects specifically related to
Childe Harold (III.lv.1):

> The castled crag of Drachenfels
> Frowns o'er the wide and winding Rhine,
> Whose breast of waters broadly swells
> Between the banks which bear the vine.

One of the finest of Turner's designs for the Finden series,
this view unites the splendid scenery of this stretch of the
Rhine with a lively account of the human and commercial activity of the river. Turner could refer to his material
from his Rhine tour of 1817 (see no.86), and this view is
essentially a reversal of another watercolour from the series made that year and acquired by Walter Fawkes
(Private Collection; W 666). Here the convent island appears on the right, with Roland's Arch on the hill behind.
These sites were powerfully associated with the 'Chanson
de Roland', telling the tale of the brave knight and his
lover who, believing him dead in battle, took orders only
to find he had returned. Moved by these sad echoes,
Byron's Harold gives way to desperate yearnings for his
own lost love at this point of his journey along the Rhine.
Turner was later to return to this spot, and to the story of
Roland, when illustrating the poems of Thomas Campbell
in 1837.

WILLIAM FINDEN (1787–1852) AFTER
J.M.W. TURNER

54 **The Drachenfels** 1833
Line-engraving, published state (R 42)
86 × 132 (3³/₈ × 5³/₁₆) on plain paper
100 × 134 (3¹⁵/₁₆ × 5¹/₄); cut within plate-mark
Engraved inscriptions: 'Drawn by J.M.W. Turner,
R.A.' below image bottom left, 'Engraved by
W. Finden' below image bottom right, 'THE
DRACHENFELS' below image at centre
T06180

This was one of only two plates (the other being 'Rhodes',
no.55) engraved for *Landscape Illustrations* or for *Life and
Works* by William Finden; his plate has beautifully expressed the effect of shimmering light over the river and
the rising moon that are such striking features of Turner's
watercolour.

WILLIAM FINDEN (1787–1852) AFTER
J.M.W. TURNER

55 **Rhodes** 1833
Line engraving, published state (R 411)
86 × 130 (3³/₈ × 5¹/₈) on plain paper
102 × 133 (4 × 5¹/₄); cut within plate-mark
Engraved inscriptions: 'Drawn by J.M.W. Turner,
R.A.' below image bottom left, 'Engraved by
W. Finden' below image bottom right, 'RHODES'
below image at centre
T06179

Turner's watercolour (w 1215) is in the Yale Center for
British Art, New Haven. The plate was first published in
Finden's *Landscape Illustrations*, part xv, 1833. Its Byronic
relevance eluded Brockedon when he came to introduce
it in his annotations to the series; neither poetry nor poet
are mentioned, and there is only a brief account of the history of the Colossus of Rhodes. Turner's working drawing
was supplied by William Page.

56 Finden's Illustrations of the Life and Works of Lord Byron. With Original and Selected Information on the Subjects of the Engravings
By W. Brockedon
London, John Murray, 1833
Vol.II, open at engraving by Edward Finden (1791–1857) after J.M.W. Turner, 'The Tomb of Cecilia Metella' (R 410)
157 × 234 (6⅛ × 9³/₁₆)
Dr Jan Piggott

Brockedon, one of Murray's authors and an acquaintance of Turner, was commissioned by the publisher to provide accompanying text for Finden's *Landscape Illustrations* following Hobhouse's failure or refusal to supply copy that was at first expected (see Introduction). A text was considered necessary as – partly owing to Hobhouse's own advice – not all the subjects set to Turner and other contributors were taken from Byron's poetry, but related to episodes in his life. 'The Tomb of Cecilia Metella', however, refers to *Childe Harold* IV.xcix–cv, where the Childe reflects on the mysterious tomb-turned-fort and speculates on its ancient occupant:

> There is a stern round tower of other days,
> Firm as a fortress, with its fence of stone.

Brockedon's exposition of the subject is characteristically lazy, consisting mainly of a long extract from Hobhouse's own *Historical Illustrations to Childe Harold*. He merely adds – justly – that this view 'is one of the most beautiful that has been given in these "Illustrations", and is taken from near the church of San Sebastiano. The tomb is seen on the high ground in the Appian Way. In the middle distance, on the left, some arches appear; they formed one end of the boundary of the circus of Caracalla'. Turner's design assimilates the picturesque life of modern Rome – represented by the *contadini* figures and the overgrown walls of a garden on the right – into a panoramic view of the outskirts of the city. The original watercolour is in the City Art Gallery, Manchester (W 1214). The plate was first published in *Landscape Illustrations*, part XVI, in 1833.

57 Finden's Landscape Illustrations
Part XX, open at 'Cephalonia' 1833
Line-engraving by Edward Finden (1791–1857) after J.M.W. Turner, published state (R 413)
88 × 135 (3½ × 5⁵/₁₆) on india paper laid on wove paper 237 × 302 (9½ × 11¹⁵/₁₆); plate-mark 178 × 235 (7 × 9⁵/₁₆)
Engraved inscriptions: 'Drawn by J.M.W. Turner R.A. from a sketch by W. Page' below image bottom left, 'Engraved by E. Finden' below image bottom right, 'CEPHALONIA' and 'London, Published 1833, by J. Murray, & Sold by C. Tilt, 86 Fleet Street" below image at centre
Private Collection

Turner's watercolour (W 1217) has not been located. It was based on a drawing by William Page. The view is of Argostoli, with its causeway and bridge over the fjord, built by the British in 1813, and the Black Mountains beyond. The largest of the Ionian islands, Cephalonia is mountainous, and famed for its bright, reverberent light. It was under neutral British administration, presided over by the Peninsular hero, Colonel Napier, when Byron stayed there in 1823, planning his campaign in the war for Greek independence. Turner's view, with its lush vegetation and prominent British construction, might almost have been intended as a contrast to the plate of 'Negropont' (no.58), which showed a place known for its insanitary conditions, poor climate and unpleasant Turkish inhabitants. Byron spent nearly five months on Cephalonia, becoming increasingly disillusioned with the people he had come to assist, and bored with the place: 'There is nothing very attractive here to divide my attention; but I must attend to the Greek cause, both from honour and inclination'.

EDWARD FINDEN (1791–1857) AFTER
J.M.W. TURNER

58 **Negropont** 1834
Line-engraving, reprint published by A. Fullarton
(R 414)
85 × 132 (3⁵/₁₆ × 5³/₁₆) on plain paper
118 × 139 (4⁵/₈ × 5¹/₂); cut within plate-mark
Engraved inscriptions: 'Drawn by J.M.W. Turner,
R.A. from a sketch by T. Allison Esq.' below image
bottom left, 'Engraved by E. Finden' below image
bottom right, 'NEGROPONT' and 'A Fullarton & Co
London & Edinburgh' below image at centre
T06181

Turner's watercolour (W 1218) is in a private collection.
The plate was first published in Finden's *Landscape Illustrations*, part XXIII, 1834. Based on a drawing by Thomas
Allason, this view of the island and town of Egripo off the
coast of Evvoia (Euboea) has a somewhat peripheral
Byronic interest. The town then had a bad reputation for
dirt, disease and cruelty, and Byron's main words on the
subject had been to repeat the contemporary tradition
that the Turks of Egripo were the worst of their race.
Brockedon could only say that the view had been included
'to convey a more just idea of the fine situation of the
town, and the character of the surrounding scenery on the
shores of Euboea'. A closer view of the town with its
bridge and Venetian fort was engraved for the *Illustrations*
by William Finden after Clarkson Stanfield. Most probably Hobhouse originally had some private particulars to
impart, and indeed in his own travel writings described a
short tour to the island on which Byron was unable to accompany him, so that he was deprived of one 'who, to
quickness of observation and ingenuity of remark, united
that gay good humour which keeps alive the attention
under the pressure of fatigue, and softens the aspect of
every difficulty and danger'.

59 **The Works of Lord Byron: with his Letters
and Journals, and his Life, by Thomas
Moore, Esq.**
London, John Murray, Albemarle Street, 1832–1834
12 volumes of 17
Private Collection
[Not illustrated]

Turner's own set of the series to which, with other artists,
he had contributed vignette frontispieces and title pages.
The edition was published in monthly parts from January
1832 until April 1833; the final volume appeared in June
1833. When the first volume appeared, only fourteen volumes were announced. See Introduction and no.45 for
further notice of the series, and nos.62, 68, 72, 74, 81 for
the other volumes from Turner's set, open to display
plates after his design.

EDWARD FINDEN (1791–1857) AFTER
J.M.W. TURNER

60 **Santa Maria della Spina, Pisa** 1832
Line engraving, vignette, large paper proof of
published state (R 415)
approx. 90 × 84 (3⁹/₁₆ × 3⁵/₁₆) on plain paper
278 × 206 (10¹⁵/₁₆ × 8¹/₈); plate-mark 232 × 178
(9³/₁₆ × 7)
Engraved inscriptions: '*Drawn by J.M.W. Turner R.A.
from a sketch by W. Page*' below image, bottom left,
'*Engraved by E. Finden*' below image bottom right, 'STA

MARIA DELLA SPINA. *Pisa'* and *'London. Published by John Murray, Albemarle Str. May 1 1832'* below image at centre
T06182

Turner's watercolour (W 1219) is in the Ashmolean Museum, Oxford. It formerly belonged to Ruskin, who paid fifty guineas for it. The plate was first published as the frontispiece-vignette to vol.v of *Life and Works*, in May 1832, and appeared again in Finden's *Landscape Illustrations*, part v. In *Life and Works* v the subject introduces Moore's account of Byron's residence in Pisa in 1821–2, and the poet's letters from the city. Although Turner had himself visited Pisa and drawn this very building (see no.61), his design was based on a drawing by William Page; Murray's accounts cite £28 7s. paid for watercolour and drawing. Finden's engraving has splendidly interpreted the effect of suffusing light over the river Arno that in Turner's watercolour throws the picturesque Gothic spires of Sta Maria into high relief.

Genoa and Florence sketchbook 1828

61 **Santa Maria della Spina on the River Arno**
Pencil on lined wove paper
143 × 97 (5⅝ × 3¹³⁄₁₆)
TB CCXXXIII f.55
D21519

Drawn with other sketches of Pisa on his way to Rome in 1828, this is Turner's first study of the Gothic church beside the Arno that he made the subject of one of his vignettes for the *Life and Works* of Byron (see no.60).

62 **Life and Works of Byron**
London, 1832
Vol.VII, open at frontispiece: 'The Gate of Theseus, Athens'
(R 416, later state)
165 × 100 (6½ × 4)
Private Collection

Turner's watercolour (W 1220), which formerly belonged to Ruskin, has not been located. The plate was first published in this volume of *Life and Works* in July 1832, and was used again in *Landscape Illustrations*. The author of the original drawing from which Turner worked is not credited in the lettering. It might be presumed to have been Page or Allason, but in this instance could also have been Turner's other acquaintance T.L. Donaldson, who in 1833 published *A Collection of the Most Approved Examples of Doorways from Ancient Buildings in Greece and Italy*. Murray's accounts cite payments of £28 7s. for the watercolour and drawing, and £37 5s. 6d. for the engraving. In *Life and Works* VII the subject must be related to *The Maid of Athens*, and the seated girl on the right perhaps makes the allusion clear. On the other hand the Gate stood near the Capuchin convent beneath the Acropolis where Byron lodged in 1810 – Clarkson Stanfield drew a closer view of this after a sketch by Page for *Life and Works* – and the intention may also have been to set a general scene for the poet's Athenian experiences. The Gate is seen from the side bearing the later, Roman inscription announcing that Athens is the city of Hadrian rather than of Theseus, proclaiming the first appropriation of Greece by an alien power. The parallel with the later Turkish subjugation is clear, and the city's fall from greatness is also marked by the broken metope lying in the left foreground.

(Works, XIII, p.446) read into this a deeper and wholly appropriate mythical symbolism: 'I need not hope to make the public believe that the meaning of the sunset contending with the storm is the contest of the powers of Apollo and Athene, but there is nevertheless no question as to the fact. For Turner's grasp of Homeric sentiment was complete'. The dead camel in the foreground, and the exhausted or dying traveller beside it tended by two companions, seem also the ghosts of ancient battles – perhaps even reminding us of Achilles grieving over the slain Patroclus. When Page took his drawing, Troy was not yet excavated, and the topographical substance of Turner's design is no more than a wide plain, broken by low mounds and the winding course of the Scamander river, looking out to the Hellespont and the islands of Imbros and Samothrace.

63 **Finden's Landscape Illustrations**
Part VII, open at 'The Plain of Troy', 1832
Line-engraving by Edward Finden (1791–1857) after
J.M.W. Turner, vignette, published state (R 417)
75 × 85 (2¾ × 3⅜) on india paper laid on wove
paper 296 × 235 (11⅞ × 9⁵⁄₁₆); plate-mark 235 × 177
(9³⁄₁₆ × 6¹³⁄₁₆)
Engraved inscriptions: *'Drawn by J.M.W. Turner, R.A.
from a Sketch by W. Page'* below image bottom left,
'Engraved by E. Finden' below image bottom right,
'THE PLAIN OF TROY' and *'Published by John Murray,
Albemarle Street, 1832'* below image at centre
Private Collection

Turner's watercolour (W 1221) was in Sotheby's sale, 16 July 1987. It formerly belonged to Ruskin, who judged it 'one of the very finest of the Byron vignettes', even though it had 'half the sky baked out of it' during the Manchester Art Treasures Exhibition in 1857 (*Works*, ed. Cook and Wedderburn, XIII, 1904, pp.446, 343). The plate was first published as the title-vignette to vol.VII of *Life and Works*, in July 1832, and was used again in the *Landscape Illustrations* (shown here in one of the impressions on india paper issued in royal quarto parts). Turner's design was based on a drawing by William Page. Murray's accounts cite payment of £28 7s. for the watercolour and drawing, and £27 for the engraving. In *Life and Works* VII there is no specific mention of the Plain of Troy – although this site of the celebrated siege described in the *Iliad* is mentioned elsewhere in Moore's biography or in *Don Juan* – and the vignette, with its tempestuous sky, can only be related to *Stanzas Composed During a Thunderstorm*, actually set near Zitza. Turner has marvellously suggested the aura of epic conflict clinging to the bleak landscape of the Troad by his vivid effects of stormy sunset, and Ruskin

64 Finden's Landscape Illustrations

Part VIII, open at 'Bacharach. On the Rhine' 1832
Line-engraving by Edward Finden (1791–1857) after
J.M.W. Turner, vignette, published state (R 418)
90 × 84 (3⁹/₁₆ × 3⁵/₁₆) on india paper laid on wove
paper 297 × 240 (11¾ × 9½); plate-mark
232 × 178 (9³/₁₆ × 7)
Engraved inscriptions: *'Drawn by J.M.W. Turner, R.A.'*
below image bottom left, *'Engraved by E. Finden'* below
image bottom right, 'BACHARACH. *on the Rhine*' and
'Published by John Murray, Albemarle Street, 1832' below
image at centre
Private Collection

Turner's watercolour (w 1222) is in the Vassar College Art
Gallery, Poughkeepsie, New York. The plate was first published as the frontispiece vignette to vol.VIII of *Life and
Works*, in August 1832, and was used again in *Landscape
Illustrations* (shown here in one of the impressions on india
paper issued in royal quarto parts). Murray's accounts cite
payments of £31 10s. for the watercolour, and £27 10s. for
the engraving. In *Life and Works* VIII appears *Childe Harold*,
and Bacharach, although not mentioned specifically in the
Rhine passages in the third canto, is presented as typical
of the historic and picturesque towns of the middle
Rhine, to introduce the landscape of the poem. Turner
had visited Bacharach during his Rhine tour in 1817, and
has combined material from two drawings of that year
(TB CLX 61v and 64v) to produce this splendid conspectus of the town and its riverside life by moonlight. The
traceried windows of the Gothic chapel devoted to the
boy-martyr St Werner and the sturdy towers and walls of
the town stand beneath the ruins of Burg Stahleck; a vista
of the Rhine valley with more hills and castles extends to
the left; and in the foreground a passenger boat disem-
barks its passengers while another vessel is heavily loaded
with the local wine. For the vignette and associate drawings see C. Powell, *Turner's Rivers of Europe: The Rhine, Meuse
and Mosel*, Tate Gallery, London 1991, pp.112–13.

The critic of *Arnold's Magazine of the Fine Arts* found this
plate and the Roman subject published with it 'rather too
artificial, in every part there are "cunnynge deviuces" to
lure the eye, the pale moon herself is thrust into an
"Ethiop's ear" of a cloud to enhance her new-born cres-
cent. Yet withal when a giant chooses to gambol, we
cannot but be amazed – we feel no contempt for his powerful friskiness' (2 December 1832, p.154).

65 The Castle of St Angelo 1832

Watercolour
171 × 210 (6¹³/₁₆ × 8¼)
N05243

Engraved by Edward Finden, this design appeared first as
the title-vignette to vol.VIII of the *Life and Works*, in August 1832, and was used again in Finden's *Landscape
Illustrations*. Murray's accounts cite £31 .10s. for the drawing and £27 for the engraving. Turner had contributed a
very similar view of the Castel Sant' Angelo with St
Peter's beyond, to Roger's *Italy*, and together with 'The
Walls of Rome with the Tomb of Caius Sestus' (cat no.71),
this drawing is so similar in style and presentation as to
suggest that it was perhaps originally made for the earlier
project, or developed from ideas originally intended for it.
In *Life and Works* VIII it is to be connected with *Childe
Harold* IV.CLII–CLIV respectively describing the Castel
Sant' Angelo and St Peter's:

> Turn to the mole which Hadrian rear'd on high,
> Imperial mimic of old Egypt's piles
> …
> But lo! the dome – the vast and wondrous dome,
> To which Diana's marvel was a cell –
> … Majesty,
> Power, Glory, Strength, and Beauty all are aisled
> In this eternal ark of worship undefiled.

Through the motifs of the ox cart and the Punch and Judy
show, Turner has assimilated the modern life of Rome, its
labours and its pleasures, into this tribute to architecture
and antiquity. As in his design for Rogers, Turner has
somewhat conflated the view, bringing the main elements
closer together and enlarging the statues on the bridge.

Arnold's Magazine of the Fine Arts praised these as 'angeli
delle tenebre, a fit threshold to the shades of Hades'.

EDWARD FINDEN (1791–1857) AFTER
J.M.W. TURNER

66 **The Castle of St Angelo** 1832
Line-engraving, vignette, large paper proof of
published state (R 419)
approx. 68 × 86 (2¹¹/₁₆ × 3⁷/₁₆) on plain paper
296 × 218 (11¾ × 8⅝); plate-mark 232 × 178
(9³/₁₆ × 7)
Engraved inscriptions: *'Drawn by J.M.W. Turner, R.A.'*
below image bottom left, *'Engraved by E. Finden'* below
image bottom right, 'The Castle of St. Angelo.' and
'Published by John Murray, Albemarle Street, 1832' below
image at centre
T06183

67 **Corinth from the Acropolis** 1832
Watercolour and pencil
210 × 267 (8¼ × 10½)
Watermark: 'J.W.[HATMAN]'
Syndics of the Fitzwilliam Museum, Cambridge
W 1224

Engraved by Edward Finden, this design appeared first as
a frontispiece vignette to vol.x of the *Life and Works*, in
October 1832. It was based on a sketch by William Page,
and Murray's accounts cite £28 7s. for both works, and
£37 5s. 6d. for the engraving. The subject was used again
for Finden's *Landscape Illustrations*, part x, 1833. In *Life and
Works* x it sets the scene for *The Siege of Corinth*:

> yet she stands,
> A Fortress form'd to Freedom's hands
> The keystone of a land which still,
> Though fall'n, looks proudly on that hill,
> The landmark to the double tide
> That purpling rolls on either side,
> As if their waters chafed to meet …

Byron's poem was inspired by the Turkish siege of Corinth in 1715. Turner's vignette captures the spectacular
setting of Corinth, and also creates a somewhat threatening atmosphere by emphasising the surrounding
mountains; Turkish minarets are juxtaposed with the ruins
of the great Temple of Apollo, whose massive Doric columns are seen at the centre of the design.

68 Life and Works of Byron

London, 1832
Vol.x, open at frontispiece: 'Corinth (from the
Acropolis)'
(R 420, later state)
165 × 100 (6½ × 4)
Private Collection

69 Finden's Landscape Illustrations

Part xi, open at 'The Bridge of Sighs', 1832
Line-engraving by Edward Finden (1791–1857) after
J.M.W. Turner, vignette, published state (R 421)
92 × 80 (3⅝ × 3⅛) on india paper laid on wove
paper 302 × 240 (11¹⁵⁄₁₆ × 9½); plate-mark 235 × 177
(9¹³⁄₁₆ × 6¹³⁄₁₆)
Engraved inscriptions: *'Drawn by J.M.W. Turner. R.A.,
from a sketch by T. Little Esq.'* below image bottom left,
'Engraved by Edward Finden' below image bottom
right, 'THE BRIDGE OF SIGHS VENICE' and
'Published by John Murray, Albemarle Street, 1832' below
image at centre
Private Collection

Turner's watercolour (w 1225) has not been located. The
plate was first published as the frontispiece vignette to
vol.xi of *Life and Works*, in November 1832, and was used
again in *Landscape Illustrations* (shown here in one of the impressions on india paper issued in royal quarto parts). It is
unclear why Turner should have needed to work from a
sketch by another artist, having himself visited Venice.
Murray's accounts cite payments of £26 5s. for the watercolour and drawing, and £37 5s. 6d. for the engraving.
In *Life and Works* xi this subject of two lovers gliding
beneath the Bridge of Sighs by moonlight evokes the
atmosphere of *Beppo*, Byron's comedy of Venetian man-
ners in which a long absent husband returns to interrupt
his wife, who has first mistaken him for a Turk, with her
cavalier servente. The sinister connotations of the Bridge of
Sighs – although inevitably present – are here secondary
to the romantic mood; Turner may have had particularly
in mind the line form *Beppo* LXXXVII:

> The count and Laura found their boat at last,
> And homeward floated o'er the silent tide,
> Discussing all the dances gone and past.

EDWARD FINDEN (1791–1857) AFTER
J.M.W. TURNER

70 **The Bernese Alps** 1833
Line-engraving, vignette, large paper proof of
published state (R 422 III)
approx. 70 × 90 (2³⁄₄ × 3⁹⁄₁₆) on plain paper 284 ×
222 (11³⁄₁₆ × 8³⁄₄); plate-mark 234 × 178 (9³⁄₁₆ × 7)
Engraved inscriptions: *'Drawn by J.M.W. Turner, R.A.'*
below image bottom left, *'Engraved by E. Finden'* below
image bottom right, *'The Bernese Alps'* and *'Published
by John Murray, Albemarle Street, 1833'* below image
at centre
T06184

Turner's watercolour (W 1226) is in the Vassar College Art
Gallery, Poughkeepsie, New York. The plate was first published as the title-vignette to vol.XI of the *Life and Works*,
in November 1832, and was used again in Finden's *Landscape Illustrations*, part XI. In *Life and Works* XI it introduces
the Alpine setting of *Manfred*, though Turner's distant view
of the mountains, with Berne itself in the middle distance,
hardly approaches the sublimity of that poem. Murray's
accounts cite £28 7s. for the watercolour and £54 for the
engraving.

71 **The Walls of Rome with the Tomb of Caius
Sestus** 1833
Watercolour
146 × 197 (5¹³⁄₁₆ × 7¹³⁄₁₆)
W 1227
N05242

Engraved by Edward Finden, this design appeared first as
the title-vignette to vol.XIII of the *Life and Works*, in
January 1833, and was used again in Finden's *Landscape
Illustrations*, part XIII. Murray's accounts cite £31 10s. for
the drawing and a sketch, and £54 for the engraving.
Scene 2 and Part II, scene 1 of Byron's verse drama *The
Deformed Transformed*, printed in *Life and Works* XIII, take
place before the walls of Rome. Turner's design avoids the
drama of the siege envisioned in Part II, but rather the
meditation of Bourbon in the previous scene:

> but those walls have guided in great ages,
> And sent forth mighty spirits. The past earth
> And present phantom of Imperial Rome
> Is peopled with those warriors; and methinks
> They flit along the eternal city's rampart,
> And stretch their glorious, gory, shadowy hands,
> And beckon me away.

The pyramid of Cestius is not specifically mentioned by
Byron, but Turner could perhaps have been guided to set
his view of the Roman ramparts beside it, by Hobhouse
whose *Historical Illustrations to Childe Harold* compared it to
the Tomb of Cecilia Metella: 'Cestius is as little famous as
Metella, and his pyramid is no less conspicuous than her
tower'. The double lighting of moonlight and sunset – one
of Turner's favourite Byronic effects – and the group of
mourners standing beside a freshly dug grave, imbue the
scene with poignancy and sadness.

72 **Life and Works of Byron**
London, 1833
Vol.XIII, open at title-page: 'The Walls of Rome,
Tomb of Caius Sestus'
(R 423, later state)
165 × 100 (6½ × 4)
Private Collection

Watercolour and bodycolour
184 × 140 (7⁵/₁₆ × 5⁵/₈)
W 1228
N05238

Engraved by Edward Finden, this design appeared first as
the frontispiece vignette to vol.XIV of the *Life and Works*,
in February 1833, and was used again in Finden's *Landscape Illustrations*, part XIV. Murray's accounts cite £28 7s.
for the drawing, and the working sketch by William Page,
and £37 5s. 6d. for the engraving. In *Life and Works* XIV
the subject is related to the passage in *The Island* (II.xii)
where the narrator reflects on his past experiences of
North and South, when he had 'revered Parnassus' and
mingled impressions of 'Highland linns with Castalie's
clear fount'. However, a more affecting and significant
allusion to Delphi, which Turner must have considered,
comes at the very beginning of *Childe Harold*, as the poet
invokes his muse:

> Oh, thou! in Hellas deem'd of heavenly birth;
> Muse!
> …
> Mine dares not call thee from thy sacred hill;
> Yet there I've wander'd by thy vaunted rill;
> Yes! sigh'd o'er Delphi's long deserted shrine,
> Where, save that feeble fountain, all is still.

Byron's note to this, describing the village of Castri on the
slopes of Parnassus, with its deep Pythian cave and Greek
monastery, and above this a range of caverns leading into
the mountain from which descends the Castalian stream,
was surely the foundation of Turner's watercolour. The
antiquities of Delphi were then largely concealed, and the
life of the inhabitants of Castri – who washed their dirty
linen in the sacred stream – much debased. Turner could
have read of their grubby habits, as well as of the sublim-
ities of the place, in his copy of T.S. Hughes's *Travels in
Sicily, Greece and Albania* (1820), and his watercolour com-
bines both the everyday activities of modern Greece with
the splendour of mountain scenery and the sparkling
drama of air and water. 'Parnassus and Castalian Spring'
is undoubtedly among the very finest of the Byron vignettes, conveying a very Byronic contrast between past
and present, and a no less Byronic belief in the eternal
energies of nature.

Turner could have heard first-hand impressions of
Delphi and Castri from Eastlake, who had visited the site
in 1818, and found Byron's name carved in a small chapel
nearby.

74 **Life and Works of Byron**
London, 1833
Vol.XIV, open at frontispiece: 'Parnassus and
Castalian Spring'
(R 424, later state)
165 × 100 (6½ × 4)
Private Collection

EDWARD FINDEN (1791–1857) AFTER
J.M.W. TURNER

75 **The Field of Waterloo. From Hougoumont**
1833
Line-engraving, vignette, large paper proof of
published state (R 425)
approx. 53 × 95 (2⅛ × 3¾) on india paper laid on
wove paper 292 × 212 (11½ × 8⅝); plate-mark
232 × 178 (9³⁄₁₆ × 7)
Engraved inscriptions: '*Drawn by J.M.W. Turner, R.A.*'
below image bottom left, 'Engraved by E. Finden'
below image bottom right, '*The Field of Waterloo.
From Hougoumont*' and 'Published by John Murray.
Albemarle Street, 1833' below image at centre
T06185

Turner's watercolour (W 1229) has been recorded in an
American private collection, and published in detail by
R. Griffith Jones, *Turner Studies*, vol.I, no.2, 1981, p.54. The
plate was published as the title vignette to vol.XIV of *Life
and Works*, in February 1833, and used again in Finden's
Landscape Illustrations, part XIV. In *Life and Works* XIV it
illustrates a line from *The Age of Bronze* (v.222) – 'Oh,
bloody and most bootless Waterloo!' – though it could
equally have been intended to accompany the Waterloo
stanzas of *Childe Harold*. Turner has brilliantly condensed
the horrific imagery and documentary truth of his Byronic
painting of 1818 (no.35) within the small space of a vignette, and exploited the open nature of the design to
create a far more dramatic interplay of the light from fire
and flares. Here there are no women searching among the
dead as in the oil, and the focus is rather on the burning
farm of Hougoumont, which had stood as a vital bastion
against the French attack even after Napoleon's army had
blasted it with howitzers.

Murray's accounts cite £31 10s. for the drawing and a
sketch of Waterloo – though Turner can hardly have
needed the latter – and £27 for the engraving.

76 Waterloo: Cannon, Horsemen and Soldiers
Watercolour and pencil
260 × 325 (10¼ × 12¾)
TB CCLXXX 5
D27522

This large sketch for a vignette motif seems to be related to the right half of Turner's watercolour of Waterloo acquired by Walter Fawkes after Turner's visit to the battlefield in 1817 (fig.3 on p.20), with however allegorical overtones in the pencil indications of figures, hovering or rising as if in apotheosis, at upper left of the drawn area. Clearly he was continuing to think about the apocalyptic implications of the appalling carnage he had so graphically portrayed in his painting 'Field of Waterloo' (no.35) and his watercolour of the same date.

EDWARD FINDEN (1791–1857) AFTER
J.M.W. TURNER

77 Scio (Fontana di Melek Mehmet, Pasha) 1833
Line-engraving, vignette, large paper proof of
published state (R 426)
approx. 85 × 80 (3⅜ × 3³⁄₁₆) on plain paper
286 × 212 (11⅝ × 8⅝); plate-mark 232 × 178
(9³⁄₁₆ × 7)
Engraved inscriptions: *'Drawn by J.M.W. Turner, R.A.
from a sketch by W. Page'* below image bottom left,
'Engraved by E. Finden' below image bottom right,
'SCIO (Fontana dé Melek Mehmet, Pasha)' and,
'Published by John Murray, Albemarle Street, 1833' below
image at centre
T06186

Turner's watercolour (W 1230) was in the collection of Ruskin, who believed it to be a view in Constantinople – presumably the Tophané fountain. It was in Sotheby's sale, 10 July 1986. The plate was first published as the frontispiece vignette to vol.XV of the *Life and Works*, in March 1833, and used again in Finden's *Landscape Illustrations*. The subject can only be loosely associated with Byron's allusions to 'Scio's muse' (Homer) and 'Scio's vine' in the song to Greek liberty in *Don Juan* III.lxxxvi.2, 9 – although in this context the prominence given to the Turkish fountain, and the leisurely posture of the two Turks on the right contrasted with the Greek girls carrying water and the elderly woman slumped on the left, become powerfully ironic. Murray's account cites £31 10s. for the drawing and Page's sketch, and £37 5s. 6d. for the engravings. For another Scio subject, and for Byron on Ithaca in 1823, see no.82.

EDWARD FINDEN (1791–1857) AFTER
J.M.W. TURNER

78 **Genoa**
Line-engraving, vignette, large paper proof of
published state (R 427)
approx. 60 × 100 (2⁵/₁₆ × 3⁷/₈) on plain paper
292 × 211 (11¹/₂ × 8⁵/₁₆); plate-mark 232 × 178
(9³/₁₆ × 7)
Engraved inscriptions: '*Drawn by J.M.W. Turner, R.A.*'
below image bottom left, '*Engraved by E. Finden*' below
image bottom right, '*Genoa*' and '*Published by John
Murray, Albemarle Street, 1833*' below image at centre
T06188

Turner's watercolour (W 1231) is in a private collection.
The plate was first published as the title-vignette to vol.xv
of the *Life and Works*, in March 1833, and was used again
for Finden's *Landscape Illustrations*, part xv. In *Life and
Works* xv it can only be related to Don Juan's voyage to
'the port Leghorn' (*Don Juan*, 11.xxiv). On the other hand
Byron's last months in Italy were spent in or near Genoa,
and Turner's distant view of the city from the sea with
boats in the foreground and a ship putting out of the harbour may originally have been intended to evoke the
poet's last sight of Italy, and his departure for Cephalonia
and his Greek campaign (see also no.57). Murray's accounts cite £31 10s. for the watercolour, and £37 5s. 6d.
for the engravings.

EDWARD FINDEN (1791–1857) AFTER
J.M.W. TURNER

79 **Cologne** 1833
Line engraving, vignette, large paper proof of
published state (R 428)
approx. 81 × 78 (3³/₁₆ × 3¹/₈) on wove paper
263 × 202 (10⁷/₁₆ × 8); plate-mark 232 × 178
(9³/₁₆ × 7)
Engraved inscriptions: '*Drawn by J.M.W. Turner, R.A.*'
below image bottom left, '*Engraved by E. Finden*' below
image bottom right, 'COLOGNE' and '*Published by
John Murray, Albemarle Street, 1833*' below image
at centre
T06189

Turner's watercolour (W 1232) was on the London art
market in 1978. The plate was first published as the frontispiece-vignette to vol.xvi of *Life and Works* in April 1833,
and appeared again in Finden's *Landscape Illustrations*, part
xvi. Murray's accounts cite a payment of £31 10s. for the
watercolour, and £27 for the engraving. Turner's design
compresses into vignette format some of the principal
buildings of Cologne, chiefly the cathedral and Great St
Martin's church, and adds vivid details of the life of the
Rhine. In *Life and Works* xvi is it to be related to *Don Juan*
x.lxii and its frivolous allusion to St Ursula and her 11,000
virgins, who (as Byron had cause to know having been in-
terrupted in a carnal adventure upon a chambermaid in
his Cologne hotel) 'were still extant in 1816':

> From thence he was drawn onwards to Cologne,
> A city which presents to the inspector
> Eleven thousand maidenheads of bone,
> The greatest number flesh has ever known.

80 **St Sophia, Constantinople** 1833
Watercolour
155 × 225 (6¹/8 × 8⁷/8)
Board of Trustees of the Victoria and Albert Museum, London
W 1233

Engraved by Edward Finden, this design appeared first as
the title-vignette to vol.XVI of the *Life and Works,* in April
1833, and was used again in Finden's *Landscape Illustrations.*
Murray's accounts cite £29 8s. for the drawing, and the
working sketch by Charles Barry; and £37 5s. 6d. for the
engraving. In *Life and Works* XVI the subject is related to
Don Juan v.iii: 'Sophia's cupola with golden gleam'.

Arnold's Magazine of the Fine Arts observed in this design
'an oriental charm...combined with a classic purity quite
in accordance with the poetical taste of Byron'.

81 **Life and Works of Byron**
London, 1833
Vol.XVI, open at title-page: 'St. Sophia,
Constantinople'
(R 429, later state)
165 × 100 (6¹/2 × 4)
Private Collection

EDWARD FINDEN (1791–1857) AFTER
J.M.W. TURNER

82 **The School of Homer (Scio)** 1833
Line-engraving, vignette (R 430)
approx. 81 × 87 (3³/₁₆ × 3¹/₈) on wove paper 263 ×
200 (10⁷/₁₆ × 7¹⁷/₁₆); plate-mark 232 × 178 (9³/₁₆ × 7)
Engraved inscriptions: '*Drawn by J.M.W. Turner, R.A.
from a sketch by W. Page*' below image bottom left,
'*Engraved by E. Finden*' below image bottom right,
'THE SCHOOL OF HOMER (Scio)' and '*London.
Published 1835, by John Murray, Albemarle Street*'
below image at centre
T06190

Turner's watercolour (W 1234) is in the Ashmolean Museum, Oxford (pl.oo). It formerly belonged to Ruskin, who
paid fifty guineas for it. The plate was first published as
the frontispiece-vignette to vol.XVII of the *Life and Works*,
in June 1833, and appeared again in Finden's *Landscape
Illustrations*, part XVII. The design was based on a drawing by William Page. Murray's accounts cite a payment of
£28 7s. for the watercolour and drawing, and £37 5s. 6d.
for the engraving. Here again the connection is more biographical than poetic, for the last of several excursions
Byron made on Ithaca in the summer of 1823 was to the
so-called 'School of Homer', one of many Mycenaean
outcrops on the island. Ironically, in emphasising the
Homeric connection, Turner has chosen the occasion of
one of Byron's most robust dismissals of 'antiquarian
twaddle' and 'poetical humbug'; '"Do I look like one of
those emasculated fogeys?"' his friend Trelawny remembered him demanding when an earnest antiquarian tour
of Ithaca's historic sites was proposed, 'Let's have a swim'.

83 **Finden's Landscape Illustrations**
Part XVII, open at 'The Castellated Rhine', 1833
Line-engraving by Edward Finden (1791–1857) after
J.M.W. Turner, vignette, published state (R 431)
approx. 73 × 97 (2⁷/₈ × 3⁷/₈) on india paper laid on
wove paper 300 × 238 (11³/₄ × 9¹/₂); plate-mark
232 × 178 (9³/₁₆ × 7)
Engraved inscriptions: '*Drawn by J.M.W. Turner R.A.*'
below bottom left, '*engraved by E. Finden*' below image
bottom right, '*The Castellated Rhine*' and '*Published by
John Murray. Albemarle Street, 1833*' below image at
centre
Private Collection

Turner's watercolour (W 1235) is in the Beit Collection.
The plate was first published as the title-vignette to
vol.XVII of *Life and Works*, in June 1833, and was used
again in *Landscape Illustrations* (shown here in one of the impressions on india paper issued in royal quarto parts).
Murray's accounts cite payments of £31 for the watercolour and £27 for the engraving. Turner's view brings
together Kaub and Burg Gutenfels on the left bank, and
Oberwesel on the right. Although placed in *Life and Works*
XVII, this splendid amalgam of the archetypal scenery
and activities of the Rhine, irradiated with light, properly
refers to *Don Juan* x.lxi, in vol.XV:

> And thence through Berlin, Dresden, and the like,
> Until he reach'd the castellated Rhine:–
> Ye glorious Gothic scenes! how much ye strike
> All phantasies, not even excepting mine!
> A grey wall, a green ruin, rusty pike,
> Make my soul pass the equinoctial line
> Between the present and past worlds, and hover
> Upon their airy confine, half-seas-over.

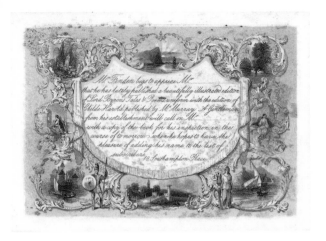

84 Trade Card of William Finden
Steel plate and impression
128 × 175 (5 × 6¹⁵/₁₆)
Inscription within decorative borders: 'Mr Finden
begs to apprize Mr   that he has lately
published a beautifully illustrated edition of Lord
Byrons Tales and Poems uniform with the edition
of Childe Harold published by Mr Murray. A
gentleman from his establishment will call on
Mr   with a copy of the book for inspection
in the course of tomorrow when he hopes to have
the pleasure of adding his name to the list of
subscribers. 18 Southampton Place'
Iain Bain

It is not certain to which of Finden's Byronic enterprises
this subscription card refers. The description of an edition
uniform with Murray's might suggest that it was the *Landscape Illustrations*, but the allusion to 'Tales and Poems' and
the romantic and figurative character of the border deco-
rations would fit better with Finden's later *Byron Gallery*, in
which Turner was not involved.

TURNER IN BYRON'S EUROPE;
OTHER WORKS

Turner's travels took him to many places visited and
described by Byron. His visit to Switzerland in 1802 actually preceded Byron's, and he saw the Low Countries,
the Rhineland and Italy with Byron's allusive and
didactic commentaries already read. Like Byron, he saw
Europe during and after the Napoleonic War, and con-
fronted the Emperor's achievement and fate, and its
lessons for the future, in his art.

85 War: The Exile and the Rock Limpet* RA 1842
Oil on canvas
795 × 795 (31¹/₄ × 31¹/₄)
Turner Bequest
B&J 400
N00529

Turner's Academy exhibits during the 1840s included a
number of retrospective meditations on Europe and its recent history. They included his various beautiful but
inescapably poignant visions of Venice, and the more op-
timistic tribute to cultural revival in Germany, 'The
Opening of the Wallhalla' (Tate Gallery; B&J 401) shown
in 1843. This picture, which in the Academy in 1842 was
paired with Turner's tribute to his late friend and fellow
painter, Sir David Wilkie, 'Peace – Burial at Sea' (Tate
Gallery; B&J 399), may be said to answer the question
posed in the verses from his *Fallacies of Hope* that Turner
appended to his Walhalla picture – 'who rode on they re-

lentless car, fallacious Hope?' The answer was of course Napoleon, whose ambition and empire-building had for so long dominated Europe and whose shadow still lay heavily on hearts and minds from his exile in St Helena. In Turner's picture, the lonely figure of Napoleon, a giant even in captivity, is contrasted with the diminutive form of a rock-limpet which, however humble, was at least free, and set against a bloodshot sky that speaks for all the carnage he had caused. Turner supplied some appropriate lines from *The Fallacies of Hope:*

> 'Ah! they tent-formed shell is like
> A soldier's nightly bivouac, alone
> Amidst a sea of blood –
> …
> but you can join your comrades.'

For many of Turner's generation, Napoleon had first appeared as a shining reformer, and making war against him had exercised the liberal conscience. It had been easier when his imperial ambitions had become more blatant, but his final defeat was no matter of celebration in that it restored reactionary and undemocratic regimes in many parts of Europe. This was Byron's position, and his vivid pictures of war-torn Europe in *Childe Harold* and penetrating satire on the peace in *The Age of Bronze* are deeply critical of the post-Napoleonic order. Similar views were passionately held by the painter B.R. Haydon, whose numerous and popular versions of a picture of Napoleon musing on St Helena – one of which belonged to Samuel Rogers – may have helped to inspire Turner's canvas. Turner's opinions were probably less biased, and his picture is best seen as an attempt to exorcise a still potent force – one that had determined the course of the history of his time, and still aroused difficult and ambivalent emotions.

86 **Drachenfels** 1817
Watercolour and bodycolour on white paper prepared with grey wash
209 × 290 (8¼ × 11⅜)
Courtauld Institute Galleries, London (Spooner Bequest 1967)
w 667

Turner's Rhine tour in 1817, following his visit to the field of Waterloo, may well have been prompted in part by his reading of *Childe Harold* III, with its vivid and affecting descriptions of the scenery and history of the river. Having in effect anticipated Byron in his interest in Greece and his journey to Switzerland in 1802, Turner could now travel with recollections of his poetry in mind. His interest was most probably fostered by the Byronic sympathies of Walter Fawkes, who, just as he had done with many of the finished watercolours based on the 1802 tour, acquired the fifty-one Rhine views – including this one of Drachenfels – that he made very soon after his return to England. Byron's description captures the anticipation of the traveller moving towards the wooded gorges of the river, and Turner's coach on the narrow riverside road seems to echo it. See no.53 for the view of Drachenfels made for Finden's *Landscape Illustrations* to Byron.

87 Ehrenbreitstein, during the Demolition of the Fortress 1819–20
Watercolour and scraping-out
180 × 286 (7$^{1}/_{8}$ × 11$^{5}/_{16}$)
Bury Art Gallery and Museum
W 687

Engraved in 1824 by J.C. Allen (R 202), and based on material from his 1817 tour of the Rhine, this, together with a larger watercolour also at Bury (W 1051) shows the fortress at Ehrenbreitstein being blown up by the Prussians, prior to its rebuilding between 1815 and 1832. Both these views also show the striped pontoon of the old flying bridge between Coblenz and Ehrenbreitstein, which in 1819 was replaced by a bridge of boats. Like Byron, who wrote in *Childe Harold* III.lviii of

> Ehrenbreitstein, with her shatter'd wall
> Black with the miner's blast

and saw it in 1816 as 'a ruin', Turner has preserved the memory of the fortress as it was immediately after the war, before it was reconstructed. This watercolour was again engraved, on a reduced scale, for the *Literary Souvenir*, 1828 (R 317a); this second plate was by John Pye, for whom Turner painted his Byronic oil of Ehrenbreitstein, 'The Bright Stone of Honour ... from Byron's "Childe Harold" ' (see p.93).

88 Brüderberggen on the Rhine 1817
Watercolour and bodycolour on white paper prepared with grey wash
212 × 330 (8$^{3}/_{8}$ × 13)
Syndics of the Fitzwilliam Museum, Cambridge
W 651

Another example of the series of Rhine views acquired by Walter Fawkes just after Turner's Rhine tour in 1817. Byron had made much of the ruined castles overlooking the Rhine in *Childe Harold* III; Turner's view shows two of them, Sterrenberg and Libenstein, known as the Brüderberggen, above the convent of Bornhofen, on the east bank of the Rhine near Kamp. The name commemorates the legend of the brothers Konrad and Heinrich, sons of Bayer von Boppard, and their love for Hildegarde.

89 **Coblenz** 1844
  Watercolour, pen and pencil
  228 × 329 (8¹⁵/₁₆ × 13)
  TB CCCLII 19
  D35239

A light and airy sketch, pulled together by deft touches of red, from Turner's *Rhine and Rhine Castles* sketchbook used in 1844. Ehrenbreitstein (for which see p.93 and no.87) towers over the town.

90 **Avenches, the Town and the Ruined Column, 'Le Cicognier'**
  Pencil, black and white chalks on brownish grey paper
  210 × 284 (8¼ × 11³/₁₆)
  Inscribed bottom right: 'Avanches'
  TB LXXIV 95
  D04588

Avenches, near Morat, stands on the site of the Roman city of Aventicum, capital of Helvetia. The single Corinthian column, part of a Roman temple of Apollo, was long known as 'Le Cicognier' from the generations of storks who built their nests on top of it. Byron described it in *Childe Harold* III.lxv:

By a lone wall a lonelier column rears
A gray and grief-worn aspect of old days;
'Tis the last remnant of the wreck of years,
And looks as with the wild-bewilder'd gaze
Of one to stone converted by amaze,
Yet still with consciousness; and there it stands
Making a marvel that it not decays,
When the coeval pride of human hands,
Levell'd Adventicum, hath strew'd her subject lands.

Turner drew Avenches in 1802, in a series of monochrome studies assigned to a 'Grenoble' sketchbook on the basis of the numerous drawings of that town contained within it.

91 **Chillon** 1841
Watercolour and pencil
228 × 293 (8^{15}/$_{16}$ × 11^{1}/$_{2}$)
Watermark: J WHATMAN/TURKEY MILL/1841
TB CCCXXXII 13
D33483

A sheet from Turner's *Fribourg, Lausanne and Geneva* sketch-book used in 1841. Turner made a number of watercolours of Chillon, which he first saw in 1802. His views invari-ably concentrate on the idyllic setting of the castle by the Lake of Geneva, but he would have absorbed the heroic and tragic history of the castle into his perception of the place, as all Romantic travellers did. Here the invading Duke of Savoy had imprisoned the Genevan patriot Bonnivard, so that the castle had become an icon and a shrine to Liberty.

Byron visited the castle twice in 1816, first with Shelley, whom he had recently met for the first time at Sécheron, and later that summer with Hobhouse. He considered it 'the most anti-narcotic spot in the world' (and was thus shocked to encounter an English lady asleep in her car-riage), while Mary Shelley, after her own tour of the dungeons of the castle, shivered at the memory of 'that cold and inhuman tyranny, which it has been the delight of man to exercise over man'. Byron told the story of Bonnivard in his *Prisoner of Chillon* (1816) and prefaced it with his fine sonnet beginning

> Eternal Spirit of the chainless Mind!
> Brightest in Dungeons, Liberty! thou art.

The heroic captive, shackled in his gloomy dungeon, be-came a favourite subject for popular illustrators of Byron (see no.18).

92 **Lausanne and Lake Geneva*** 1841
Pencil, watercolour and pen
236 × 334 (9^{5}/$_{16}$ × 13^{3}/$_{16}$)
TB CCCXXXIV 4
D33528

A sheet from Turner's *Lausanne* sketchbook used in 1841. Turner often returned late in life to this view of Lake Geneva from the steep slopes of Lausanne to the Savoy mountains. To the spectacular natural setting and its con-stant changes of light was added the recollection of the literary associations of the place, familiar to all cultured travellers. The summer-house in Lausanne where Edward Gibbon had written his *Decline and Fall of the Roman Empire* was a popular place of pilgrimage, and Rousseau had set his novel *La Nouvelle Heloïse* in the same area; Voltaire had lived at Ferney; and Madame de Staël held her salon at Coppet. Byron took the Villa Diodati, at Geneva, in the summer 1816, and Shelley was also living nearby at the Maison Chappuis. Byron, who of course had added his own lustre to the lake by the time Turner returned to it in the 1840s, paid tribute to its literary presences in his *Sonnet to Lake Leman*, written at Diodati in 1816:

> Rousseau – Voltaire – our Gibbon – and De Staël –
> Leman! these names are worthy of thy shore,
> Thy shore of names like these! wert thou no more,
> Their memory thy remembrance would recall:
> …
> How much more, Lake of Beauty! do we feel,
> In sweetly gliding o'er thy crystal sea,
> The wild glow of that not ungentle zeal,
> Which of the heirs of immortality
> Is proud, and makes the breath of glory real!

Turner would certainly have incorporated such reflections in his response to the lake, and added Byron and Shelley to its past associations, but his watercolour dwells instead on the contemporary reality, as Ruskin observed: 'a car-riage and four driving down on the left, one postillion only, in the foreign fashion … The walk in front of us is one of the favourite resorts of the townspeople; a nurse with two children is sketched on the left' (*Ruskin on Pictures*, ed. E.T. Cook, 1902, p.120).

94 Geneva: The Mole and Savoy Hills 1841
Pencil and watercolour
228 × 295 ($9^{1}/_{16}$ × $11^{5}/_{8}$)
TB CCCXXXII 8
D33478

A sheet from the *Fribourg, Lausanne and Geneva* sketchbook used in 1841. From Geneva itself the view of the Lake is somewhat confined, and the mountains beyond seem tamed of their sublimity. Turner's views of the lake from the town often breathe a transcendental calm, echoing Byron's sentiments in *Childe Harold* III.lxxxv:

> Clear, placid Leman! thy contrasted lake,
> With the wild world I dwelt in, is a thing
> Which warns me, with its stillness, to forsake
> Earth's troubled waters for a purer wing
> To waft one from distraction.

93 Geneva, the Jura Mountains and Isle Rousseau, Sunset 1841
Watercolour and pencil
228 × 293 ($8^{15}/_{16}$ × $11^{1}/_{2}$)
TB CCCXXXII 9
D33479

A sheet from Turner's *Fribourg, Lausanne and Geneva* sketchbook used in 1841.

95 **Genoa from the Sea** *c.*1828
Watercolour, bodycolour and pen on grey paper
139 × 190 (5½ × 7½)
TB CCLIX 213
D24778

In 1828 Turner travelled to Italy by sea, along the Mediterranean coast from Marseilles to Genoa, recording in vividly coloured studies on blue paper a shore-line that he told his friend George Jones was 'remarkably rugged and fine' (Gage, *Correspondence*, no.141). Pencil sketches of the harbour of Genoa, dominated by its tall lighthouse, also occur in Turner's *Marseilles to Genoa* and *Coast of Genoa* sketchbooks (TB CCXXXI, CCXXXII). The vignette of Genoa subsequently made for the *Life and Works* of Byron (see no.78) may be partly descended from this drawing.

Byron spent his last months in Italy, in the winter of 1822–3, in the Casa Saluzzo at Albaro, in the suburbs of Genoa. It was in Genoa that he planned his final expedition to Greece, sailing first to Cephalonia (see no.57). In January 1834 – too late to help Turner with his research for his illustrations – there appeared in *Blackwood's Magazine* (XXXV) an article 'Voyage from Leghorn to Cephalonia with Lord Byron' by a travelling companion, James Hamilton Browne, who had volunteered himself for the Greek cause.

96 **Venice: Looking East from the Giudecca – Early Morning*** 1819
Watercolour
222 × 287 (8¾ × 11⅜)
TB CLXXXI 5
D15255

The few days Turner spent in Venice during his first visit to Italy in 1819 were a revelation. His watercolours of the city represent a fresh departure in his art, and a new understanding of the expressive power of the medium. Working directly with the brush without any preliminary indications in pencil, using very dilute washes and leaving the white paper to shine through and co-ordinate the tonal patterns, he has created here a marvellous evocation of the city at sunrise, and a perfect match for Byron's second stanza in *Childe Harold* IV:

> She looks a sea Cybele, fresh from ocean,
> Rising with her tiara of proud towers
> At airy distance, with majestic motion,
> A ruler of the waters and their powers.

Byron was living in Venice in 1819, and it has sometimes been suggested that Turner could have met him there – perhaps through Richard Belgrave Hoppner, the British consul, who was a friend and confidant of Byron and the son of Turner's fellow painter, John Hoppner. However, Byron's relationship with the Countess Guiccioli was keeping him almost entirely at his villa outside the city, La Mira on the Brenta river, and had moreover brought a temporary coolness in his friendship with Hoppner, while Turner must have wished to reserve all his time for his work and for discovering the city. No doubt, however, Turner spared a second look for Byron's Venetian residence, the Palazzo Mocenigo on the Grand Canal (see no.8).

97 **Venice: The Campanile of St Mark's and the Doge's Palace** 1819
Pencil and watercolour
225 × 289 (9⁷⁄₈ × 11³⁄₈)
TB CLXXXI 7
D15258

This is Turner's earliest account of the classic view towards the Piazzetta from the Bacino, familiar from pictures by Canaletto, which was to form part of his first exhibited Venetian oil in 1833, and appear again in his painting 'Venice, the Bridge of Sighs' (no.38), shown in 1840 with a version of Byron's line from *Childe Harold* IV.i:

> I stood in Venice, on the Bridge of Sighs;
> A palace and a prison on each hand.

98 **A Bedroom in Venice** *c.*1840
Watercolour and bodycolour on grey paper
230 × 302 (9¹⁄₈ × 11⁷⁄₈)
Inscribed on verso: 'J M W T Bedroom at Venice' and 'F' (?)
TB CCCXVII 34
D32219

This airy interior, its windows looking towards the Campanile of St Mark's, is presumably Turner's bedroom at the Hotel Europa on the Grand Canal, where he stayed in the late summer of 1840. Its vividness and immediacy, suggesting the joyousness of a sunny morning and a tumbled untidiness of bedding and clothing may be contrasted with the contrived theatricality of William Lake Price's view of Byron's room in the Palazzo Mocenigo (no.9).

99 **Venice, the Arsenal*** *c.*1840
Watercolour and bodycolour
243 × 308 (9⅝ × 12½)
TB CCCXVI 27
D32164

The Venetian Arsenal (which gave its name, based on the Arabic *Dar Sina 'a*, meaning 'House of Construction', to dockyards and ammunition stores around the world) was the centre for the city's ship-building and fleet provisioning. When Venice was at the zenith of her maritime power, Dante recorded that 16000 men were employed in the Arsenal. By the time Turner visited Venice, the workforce had dwindled along with the economy and status of the city. At the close of the Napoleonic war, when the Austrians retook the city, the fleet was no longer seaworthy and in 1822, Byron's friend Hobhouse numbered the workmen in the Arsenal at a mere 250. Such powerful proof of the decline of Venice cannot have been lost on Turner, and indeed his copy of Thomas Roscoe's *Tourist in Italy ...*, 1830 (see no.8), would have told him that 'At present, the Arsenal serves only as a spectacle to strangers, and a monument to the fallen glory of Venice'. Byron had written powerfully of the fall of Venice in *Childe Harold* and in his *Ode on Venice* –

> Thirteen hundred years
> Of wealth and glory turn'd to dust and tears;
> And every monument the stranger meets,
> Church, palace, pillar, as a mourner greets.

– and for painter and poet such reflections were inextricably mixed with more joyous response to the sheer beauty of the city.

100 **Venice: The Piazzetta and St Mark's, Night**
*c.*1833–5
Watercolour and bodycolour on brown paper
150 × 228 (5⅞ × 9)
TB CCCXVIII I
D32220

One of twenty-nine Venetian drawings in watercolour and bodycolour on brown paper usually dated to 1833 but perhaps made as late as 1835 (see Anne Lyles, *Turner: The Fifth Decade*, Tate Gallery, 1992, cat.nos.42–8). Of all Turner's Venetian subjects these are among the most Byronic, evoking the internal life of the city, often by night, its entertainments and its romantic or literary background, rather than its airy, vaporous distances. The strong, Rembrandtesque chiaroscuro of these drawings is matched in their moods, which shift from the joy and exuberance of theatrical or carnival scenes, through the more meditative and solemn atmosphere of religious worship, to the sinister or threatening gloom of narrow canals.

Both Turner and Byron knew Venice only under Austrian control. With Lombardy and the Veneto, the city had been annexed to the Austrian Empire at the Congress of Vienna in 1815. The subject state of the city is evident here in the Austrian sentry-box and the soldier on duty by a cannon outside the ducal palace: Turner has doubtless done no more than observe contemporary fact – Ruskin would later complain of the Austrian guards spoiling the symmetry of the palace arcades – but the inevitable contrast between the city's past and its debased present makes this a thoroughly Byronic image.

101 **Ruins in Rome: View from the Palatine** 1819
Watercolour and pencil
234 × 369 (9³/₁₆ × 14⁷/₁₆)
TB CLXXXIX 30
D16356

In *Childe Harold* iv.lxxviii Byron had cast his hero's petty sufferings into perspective by comparing them to the more sublime tragedy of Rome itself, proclaimed by the ruins:

> Oh Rome! my country! city of the soul!
> The orphans of the heart must turn to thee,
> Lone mother of dead empires! …
> What are our woes and sufferance? Come and see
> The cypress, hear the owl, and plod your way
> O'er steps of broken thrones and temples, Ye!
> Whose agonies are evils of a day –
> A world is at our feet as fragile as our clay.

Turner's drawing, from his *Rome Colour Studies* sketchbook used in 1819, catches the combined sense of awe and desolation felt by all Romantic visitors to Rome.

102 **Rome: The Forum with a Rainbow*** 1819
Pencil, watercolour and bodycolour on white paper prepared with grey wash
229 × 366 (9¹/₈ × 14³/₄)
TB CLXXXIX 46
D16375

The Forum, the ancient centre of Byron's 'Roman globe', was of all the city's tumbled ruins the most potent reminder of fallen greatness and vanished power, and here Gibbon had first conceived his *Decline and Fall of the Roman Empire*. Byron, in *Childe Harold*, linked his successive images of departed grandeur by the unifying light of the moon – implying the night, both beautiful and melancholy, which history had cast over modern Italy. In his Byronic painting 'Modern Rome', itself a view of the Forum (no.37), Turner adopted Byron's image of gathering dusk, 'The moon is up, and yet it is not night'; here the rainbow, doubtless observed spontaneously from nature, nevertheless reinforces the Byronic notion of the turning wheel of history, which as the poet observed in *Childe Harold* iv, had only recently brought forth Napoleon – 'one vain man, who is not in the grave' – to succeed the all-conquering Caesars of old:

> for this the tears
> And blood of earth flow on as they have flow'd,
> An universal deluge, which appears
> Without an ark for wretched man's abode,
> And ebbs but to reflow! Renew they rainbow, God!

While we need not suggest that Turner recollected these lines as he drew this view of the Forum after a storm, such mingled thoughts of the passage of time, of decay, and the ever renewing power of nature would have operated as much upon his mind as upon Byron's as he surveyed the relics of an ancient empire transfigured by the elements.

103 The Colosseum by Moonlight* 1819
Watercolour, bodycolour and pencil on paper
prepared with a grey wash
232 × 369 (9⅛ × 14⅜)
TB CLXXXIX 13
D16339

A sheet from Turner's *Rome Colour Studies* sketchbook used
in 1819. Viewing the Colosseum at night, by moonlight or
torchlight, was a favourite occupation of Romantic visitors
to Rome. Turner's drawing beautifully captures the pale,
silvery glimmer of the moon, the pattern of shadows cast
by the ruins and the other worldly atmosphere that Byron
celebrated in *Childe Harold* IV.cxxviii–cxxix:

> Arches on arches! as it were that Rome,
> Collecting the chief trophies of her line,
> Would build up all her triumphs in one dome,
> Her Coliseum stands; the moonbeams shine
> As 'twere its natural torches, for divine
> Should be the light which streams here to illume

> This long-explored but still exhaustless mine
> Of contemplation; and the azure gloom
> Of an Italian night, where the deep skies assume
> Hues which have words, and speak to ye of Heaven,
> Floats o'er this vast and wondrous monument,
> And shadows forth its glory.

Still more beautifully, the doomed Manfred, looking upon
the Alpine night in the hours before his death, recalls his
own erstwhile musings in the moonlit Colosseum:

> I do remember me, that in my youth,
> When I was wandering, – upon such a night
> I stood within the Coliseum's wall
> 'Midst the chief relics of almighty Rome;
> The trees which grew along the broken arches
> Waved dark in the blue midnight, and the stars
> Shone through the rents of ruin;
> …
> But the gladiators' bloody circus stands,
> A noble wreck in ruinous perfection
> …
> And thou didst shine, thou rolling moon, upon
> All of this, and cast a wide and tender light,
> Which soften'd down the hoar austerity
> Of rugged desolation, and fill'd up,
> As 'twere anew, the gaps of centuries;
> Leaving that beautiful which still was so,
> And making that which was not, till the place
> Became religion, and the heart ran o'er
> With silent worship of the great of old.

So perfectly does Turner's drawing match the spirit of
both these passages, that it is surely surprising that, in considering material for his Roman illustrations for the
Findens or for Murray, he did not turn to this subject.

Bibliography

All books published in London unless otherwise stated.

R. Altick, *Paintings from Books: Art and Literature in Britain, 1760–1900*, Columbus, Ohio 1985

W.A. Borst, *Lord Byron's First Pilgrimage*, Yale 1948

A. Burton and J. Murdoch, *Byron*, exh. cat., Victoria and Albert Museum 1974

Byron, *Letters and Journals*, ed. L.A. Marchand, 1973–82

G. Eggert, 'Lord Byron and Napoleon', *Palaestra*, 186, Leipzig, 1933

J. Gage, 'Sind Briten heir?', Britische Kunstler in Europa im 19 Jahrhundert, *Zwei Jahrunderte englische Malerei*, exh. cat., Haus der Kunst, Munich 1978

J. Gage, 'Turner and the Greek Spirit', *Turner Studies*, vol.1 no.2, 1981, pp.14–25

L. Herrmann, *Turner Prints: The Engraved Work of J.M.W. Turner*, 1990

J.D. Jump (ed.), *Byron: A Symposium*, 1975

L.A. Marchand, *Byron: A Biography*, 1957

D.L. Moore, *The Late Lord Byron*, 1961

T. Moore, *Letters and Journals of Lord Byron: With Notices of his Life*, 3rd ed., 1833

T. Moore, *Journal 1818–1841*, ed. P. Quennell, 1964

M. Omer, *Turner and the Poets*, exh. cat., Marble Hill House, Twickenham, University of East Anglia, Norwich and Central Art Gallery, Wolverhampton, undated

L. Ormond, 'Turner and Byron in Switzerland', *The Byron Journal*, 1978, pp.98–100.

C. Powell, *Turner in the South: Rome, Naples, Florence*, 1987

C. Powell, *Turner's Rivers of Europe: The Rhine, Meuse and Mosel*, exh. cat., Tate Gallery 1991

D. Robertson, *Sir Charles Eastlake and the Victorian Art World*, Princeton, 1978

S. Smiles, *A Publisher and his Friends*, 1891

W. St Clair, *That Greece Might Still Be Free: The Philhellenes in the War of Independence*, 1972

F. M. Tsigakou, *The Rediscovery of Greece: Travellers and Painters of the Romantic Era*, 1981

F. M. Tsigakou, *Byron and Greece*, exh. cat., Benaki Museum, Athens 1988

D. Watkin, *The Life and Work of C.R. Cockerell*, 1974

A. Wilton and R.M. Turner, *Painting and Poetry: Turner's 'Verse Book' and his Work of 1804–12*, exh. cat., Tate Gallery 1990

R. Woof, *Byron: A Dangerous Romantic?* exh. cat., Wordsworth Museum, Grasmere 1989–90

Jerrold Ziff, 'J.M.W. Turner on Poetry and Painting', *Studies in Romanticism*, 3, 1964, pp.207–12(a)

Jerrold Ziff, 'Turner's First Poetic Quotations: an Examination of Intention', *Turner Studies*, vol.2 no.1, 1982, pp.2–11

LENDERS

PRIVATE COLLECTIONS

Her Majesty the Queen 1
Iain Bain 84
The Earl of Elgin and Kincardine K.T. 21, 22
Lionel Lambourne 7
Dr Jan Piggott 8, 18, 56
Private Collections 2, 9, 10, 11, 12, 13, 14, 27, 28, 29, 30, 31, 32,
    41, 42, 43, 44, 45, 57, 59, 62, 63, 64, 68, 69, 72, 74, 81, 83
The Earl of Rosebery 37

PUBLIC COLLECTIONS

Bury Art Gallery and Museum 87
Burnley, Towneley Hall Art Gallery 51
Cambridge, Fitzwilliam Museum, 67, 88
London, Courtauld Institute Galleries 15, 86
London, Victoria and Albert Museum 16, 17, 80
Manchester City Art Galleries 53

Photographic Credits

Ashmolean Museum; Birmingham Museums and Art Gallery; Bury Art Gallery and Museum; Courtauld Institute; Richard L. Feigen, New York; Fitzwilliam Museum; National Portrait Gallery, London; Manchester City Art Gallery; Jack McKenzie, A.I.C. Photographic Services; Paul Mellon Centre for Studies in British Art; The Royal Collection, St James's Palace; National Galleries of Scotland; Tate Gallery Photographic Department; Towneley Hall Art Gallery and Museums; V&A Picture Library; Vouros-Etaxias Museum of the City of Athens; National Gallery of Art, Washington; John Webb

THE FRIENDS OF THE TATE GALLERY

Since their formation in 1958, the Friends of the Tate Gallery have helped to buy major works of art for the Tate Gallery Collection, from Stubbs to Hockney.

Members are entitled to immediate and unlimited free admission to Tate Gallery exhibitions with a guest, invitations to previews of Tate Gallery exhibitions, opportunities to visit the Gallery when closed to the public, a discount of 10 per cent in the Tate Gallery shop, special events, *Friends Events* and *Tate Preview* magazines mailed three times a year, free admission to exhibitions at Tate Gallery Liverpool, and use of the new Friends Room at the Tate Gallery, supported by Lloyd's of London.

Three categories of higher level memberships, Associate Fellow at £100, Deputy Fellow at £250, and Fellow at £500, entitle members to a range of extra benefits including guest cards, and invitations to exclusive special events.

The Friends of the Tate Gallery are supported by Tate & Lyle PLC.

Friends of the Tate Gallery
Tate Gallery
Millbank
London SW1P 4RG

Tel: 071-821 1313 or 071-834 2742

Tate Gallery Liverpool Supporters

Tate Gallery Liverpool Supporters were established in 1989 to promote the Gallery and help raise funds for its exhibitions and projects.

Members are entitled to unlimited free admission to Tate Gallery Liverpool and London exhibitions, invitations to private previews of Tate Gallery Liverpool exhibitions, a discount of 10 per cent on Tate Gallery Liverpool catalogues and goods in the Tate Gallery London Shop, special events, invitations to the Supporters' annual part, regular information on all Tate Gallery Liverpool activities and *Tate Preview* magazine mailed three times a year.

Further details on the Supporters may be obtained from:

Tate Gallery Liverpool Supporters
Albert Dock
Liverpool L3 4BB

Tel: 051-709 3223

PATRONS OF THE TATE GALLLERY

The Patrons of British Art support British painting and sculpture from the Elizabethan period through to the early twentieth century in the Tate Gallery's Collection. They encourage knowledge and awareness of British art by providing an opportunity to study Britain's cultural heritage.

The Patrons of New Art support contemporary art in the Tate Gallery's Collection. They promote a lively and informed interest in contemporary art and are associated with the Turner Prize, one of the most prestigious awards for the visual arts.

Annual membership ranges from £350 to £750, and funds the purchase of works of art for the Tate Gallery Collection.

Benefits for both groups include invitations to Tate Gallery receptions, an opportunity to sit on the Patrons' acquisitions committees, special events including visits to private and corporate collections and complimentary catalogues of Tate Gallery exhibitions.

Further details on the Patrons may be obtained from:

The Development Office
Tate Gallery
Millbank
London SW1P 4RG

Tel: 071-821 1313

SPONSORSHIP

Tate Gallery, London –
Sponsorships since 1989

Agfa Graphic Systems Group
  1991, *Turner: The Fifth Decade* exhibition
  and catalogue
Barclays Bank plc
  1991, *Constable* exhibition
Beck's
  1992, *Otto Dix* exhibition
British Gas plc
  1989, Education study sheets
British Gas North Thames
  1989, *Colour into Line: Turner and the Art of
  Engraving* exhibition
The British Land Company plc
  1990, *Joseph Wright of Derby* exhibition
British Petroleum Co plc
  1989, *Paul Klee* exhibition
  1990–93, *New Displays*
British Steel plc
  1989, *William Coldstream* exhibition
Carroll, Dempsey & Thirkell
  1990, *Anish Kapoor* exhibition
Channel 4 Television
  1991–93, The Turner Prize
Clifton Nurseries
  1989–91, Sponsorship in kind
Daimler Benz
  1991, *Max Ernst* Exhibition
Debenham Tewson & Chinnocks
  1990, Turner *Painting and Poetry* exhibition
Digital Equipment Co Ltd
  1991, *From Turner's Studio* touring exhibition
Drivers Jonas
  1989, *Turner and Architecture* exhibition
Erco Lighting
  1989, Sponsorship in kind
The German Government
  1992, *Otto Dix* exhibition
The Independent
  1992, *Otto Dix* exhibition
KPMG Management Consulting
  1991, *Anthony Caro: Sculpture towards
  Architecture* exhibition
Linklaters & Paines
  1989, Japanese Guide to Turner Bequest
Lin Pac Plastics
  1989, Sponsorship in kind
Lloyd's of London
  1991, Friends Room
Olympia & York
  1990, Frameworkers Conference
PA Consulting Group
  1989, Video projector
Pearsons plc
  1992–5, Elizabethan Curator Post
Reed International plc
  1990, *On Classic Ground* exhibition

SRU Ltd
  1989, Market research consultancy
  1992, *Richard Hamilton* exhibition
Tate & Lyle PLC
  1991–93, Friends relaunch marketing
  programme
TSB Group
  1992, *Turner and Byron* exhibition
  1992–5, *William Blake* series of displays
Ulster Television plc
  1989, *F.E. McWilliam* exhibition
Volkswagen
  1989–92, The Turner Scholarships
Westminster City Council
  1989, Trees project
  1989, *The Tate Gallery Companion*
  (New Display Guidebook)

Tate Gallery Liverpool –
Sponsorships since 1989

Barclays Bank plc
  1989, Sculpture for the visually impaired
BASF
  1990, *Lifelines* exhibition
Beck's Bier
  1990, *Art from Köln* exhibition
British Alcan Aluminium plc
  1991, *Dynamism* and *Giacometti* exhibitions
British Telecom
  1989, Salary for media van
  1990, Outreach Programme
Cultural Relations Committee, Department of
  Foreign Affairs, Ireland
  1991, *Strongholds* exhibition
Granada Television
  1990, *New North* exhibition
Korean Air
  1992, Sponsorship in kind
The Littlewoods Organisation plc
  1992–5, *New Realities* displays
Merseyside Development Corporation
  1989, Outreach Programme for two years
Miller & Santhouse plc
  1989, Sculpture show for visually impaired
Mobil Oil Company Ltd
  1990, *New North* exhibition
Momart plc
  1989–92, Artist-in-residence at Tate Gallery
  Liverpool
NSK Bearings Europe Ltd
  1991, *A Cabinet of Signs: Contemporary Art
  from Post Modern Japan* exhibition
Samsung Electronics
  1992, *Working with Nature* exhibition

TATE GALLERY, LONDON —
CORPORATE MEMBERS

Partners

Agfa UK Ltd
Barclays Bank plc
The British Petroleum Co plc
Glaxo Holdings plc
Manpower UK
THORN EMI
Unilever plc

Associates

Bell Helicopter Textron
Channel 4 Television
Debenham, Tewson & Chinnocks
Ernst & Young
Global Asset Management
KPMG Peat Marwick
Lazard Brothers & Co Ltd
Linklaters & Paines
Smith & Williamson
Tate & Lyle PLC
Vickers plc
S.G. Warburg Group